Museums in Beijing

中国国家汉办赠送
Donated by Hanban, China

 Foreign Languages Press

Managing editors: Lan Peijin
Text by: Zi Hui
Translated by: Ji Hua, Gao Wenxing
English text edited by: Kris Sri Bhaggiyadatta, May Yee, Wang Mingjie
Cover designed by: Wu Tao
Format designed by: Yuan Qing, et al.
Edited by: Lan Peijin

First Edition 2008

Museums in Beijing

ISBN 978-7-119-04387-6

© Foreign Languages Press
Published by Foreign Languages Press
24 Baiwanzhuang Road, Beijing 100037, China

Home Page: http://www.flp.com.cn

Distributed by China International Book Trading Corporation
35 Chegongzhuang Xilu, Beijing 100044, China
P.O. Box 399, Beijing, China

Printed in the People's Republic of China

Contents

Foreword

A museum is a palace of culture. As the finest testimony to glorious civilization and heritage, a museum preserves and displays the cultural inheritance and objective evidence of human environments. If the quantity and quality of museums in a city serves to provide a general indication of its cultural essence, then the city of Beijing should hold first place in China in this aspect.

The fertile cultural soil of Beijing comes from its illustrious history. Over many ages from about 460,000 years ago, Beijing grew from a primitive settlement into a sizable city, from being but one of many political centers in northern China, to becoming the capital of a unified feudal dynasty, until it became the capital of the People's Republic of China. Today, Beijing is an ever-expanding international cosmopolis. As the ancient capital of six imperial dynasties, Beijing has enjoyed an uninterrupted history of over 3,000 years since its formation during the ancient Yan and Ji kingdoms. A city with such a long history is rare in the world. The cultural antiques and historical artifacts bestowed by each era were passed down from one generation to the next onto the ancient land of Beijing like mighty waves adding glistening sands to a beach, turning the city of Beijing into a grand museum itself. According to statistical data, there are as many as over 130 officially registered museums in Beijing, preserving today more than 3.2 million artifacts in total. This reality moves Beijing into the ranks of developed countries, where every 100,000 to 200,000 people enjoy one museum on average. The numerous museums in Beijing have shaped the unique landscape of the city, filling this ancient capital of a great nation with an omnifarious fragrance of grace and humanism.

Beijing's museums, similar to the spread of a sumptuous buffet, may fulfil all types of tastes and all sorts of choices. Blessed by its advantageous status as the nation's capital, Beijing has gathered a great number of national museums including the National Museum of China, the Palace Museum and the National Art Museum of China, among others. The rich collections in these museums demonstrate the splendor of a great and proud country. There are also a great variety of specialty museums in Beijing, such as the China Red Sandalwood Museum, Beijing Aviation Museum, Beijing Exhibition Hall of Ancient Currencies, and the Beijing Postal Museum. Preserving every step of the developments made in the various professional fields, these specialized museums lead visitors through fascinating tunnels of space and time to explore to their hearts' content. The China Red Sandalwood Museum, for example, is praised by experts as an "encyclopedic art temple to red sandalwood." This museum, the first on red sandalwood carvings, holds the largest top-level collection of red sandalwood works in the world. Beijing also contains a great number of former residences and memorial halls of historic figures. These include those of Cao Xueqin, Lu Xun, Guo Moruo, Soong Ching Ling, Xu Beihong and Mei Lanfang. Visitors can learn more about renowned luminaries from China, and be nurtured by the unwavering spirit of human endeavor through the long river of history.

Many of Beijing's districts and counties have their own museums that also display their various unique features. The Xuan Nan Cultural Museum, for example, vividly reveals the glorious local history and rich cultural customs of the region. By viewing the exhibits, visitors learn about the colorful folk customs and modern culture of the southern Xuanwu District in old Beijing. As the number of amateur collectors keeps growing, folk museums pop up one after another in the city. The Guanfu Classic Art Museum, the first of such personal museums to sprout in Beijing, focuses its collection on cultural relics from the Ming (1368-1644) and Qing (1644-1911) dynasties.

Responding to changes over time, the museums in Beijing have focused on adding certain recreational features to their basic emphasis on knowledge learning, so that visitors can learn and have fun at the same time. The Dabaotai Western Han Dynasty Tomb Museum, in the Fengtai District of Beijing, has set up a program of "emulative archeology." Youngsters engage in simulated burial site excavations under professional guidance, to obtain a better understanding of archeology and history. Very popular among students and parents, the program is now a "big name" among Beijing museums.

A museum is yesterday's footprint of humanity, today's mirror, and tomorrow's solid stepping stone. It can be the best and the most intimate of archives, enabling humans to better understand ourselves and our environment. The dazzling panorama of Beijing's museums absorbs visitors into intriguing chapters of a vast history book, turning one page after another until they touch the innermost soul of the culture.

The National Museum of China

Location: East side of Tiananmen Square, Dongcheng District
Telephone: 65128901
Hours: 8:30-16:30 (closed on the day before Spring Festival)
Admission: 30 Yuan; students, 15 Yuan
Public Transport: Bus No. 1, 2, 4, 5, 10, 20, 22, 37, 52, & Special Route 1; Subway

The National Museum of China

Interior of an exhibition hall

The National Museum of China was originally the National History Museum, founded in 1912. It moved to its current address, from the two side buildings of Wumen Gate in the Forbidden City, in 1959 on the eve of the 10th anniversary of New China. The museum has collected more than 300,000 pieces of historical artifacts. Its time-honored Exhibition of China through History displays the growth of China from the prehistoric Yuanmou Man Age about 1.7 million years ago to the founding of the Republic of China in 1911. The museum's exhibi-

A bronze rhino wine vessel

tion space of 7,800 sq m displays over 5,000 objects, most of them being rare national treasures. (The museum, currently under renovation and repair, is still open to the public.)

A copper lamp in a human form

A painted pottery bowl with dancing figures

The Palace Museum

Location: North side of Tiananmen Square, Dongcheng District
Telephone: 65132255
Hours: April 16 - October 15: 8:30-17:00
October 16 - April 15: 8:30-16:30
Admission: 60 Yuan during high tourist season; 40 Yuan, low season
Public Transport: Bus No. 1, 2, 5, 10, 20, 22, 307
Trolley Bus No. 101, 103, 109
Subway

A pair of gilt-bronze lions outside the Heavenly Purity Gate

Overlooking the Palace Museum from the Jingshan Hill

The Palace Museum is housed in the former imperial palace of the Ming and Qing dynasties, also known as the Forbidden City. Constructed between 1407 and 1420, the imperial palace occupies 72 hectares and has more than 9,000 halls and chambers. A total of 24 emperors of the Ming and Qing dynasties had once lived here. In 1914 the "Institute for Antiques Exhibition" was established here and it

The interior of the Hall of Heavenly Purity

was renamed the "Forbidden City Museum" in 1925. More than 900,000 items of historical treasures and palace artifacts of various categories are preserved and displayed here. These categories include ceramics, treasures, clocks, paintings, bronze, jade objects, and Ming and Qing artifacts. The Palace Museum is presently the largest and the best-preserved palace complex in the world.

Jade sculpture

A gold basin with an eight-treasures design and double-phoenix ornamentation

Red sandalwood case inlaid with mother-of-pearl design of immortality greeting

The interior of the Hall of Mental Cultivation

A covered palanquin for imperial concubines in the Qing palace

A copper mirror with a design of a carriage, horses and human figures from the Eastern Han Dynasty (25-220)

A gold album that belonged to Concubine Cheng, in Han and Manchu scripts

The Hall for Worshipping Ancestors for the Qing royal family

The place where Empress Dowager Cixi held court behind a screen

The Imperial Palace of the Ming and Qing dynasties was registered on the World Heritage List in 1987.

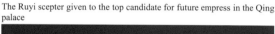

The Ruyi scepter given to the top candidate for future empress in the Qing palace

National Art Museum of China

Location: 1 Wusi Avenue, Dongcheng District
Telephone: 84033500, 64017076
Hours: 9:00-17:00
Admission: 20 Yuan
Public Transport: Bus No. 810, 812, 814
Trolley Bus No. 101, 103, 104, 108, 109, 111, 112

The National Art Museum of China is a state-level art museum specializing in the display, collection and research of modern Chinese artistic works. Equipped with exhibition halls totaling 6,000 sq. m, the museum is the most authoritative shrine to art in the nation.

An exhibition of artistic kites

The exterior of the National Art Museum of China

A calligraphy exhibition

The museum has collected over 10,000 works of modern and folk art. The exhibits also include 117 works by European and US artists. Among them are four original Picasso paintings donated by German collectors Mr. and Mrs. Ludwig. Various art exhibitions, including individual shows of fine art, are held all year round here.

The 6th National Art Exhibition of Bookbinding and Layout

Beijing Memorial Hall of the New Cultural Movement

Location: 29 Wusi Avenue, Dongcheng District
Telephone: 64020957
Hours: 9:00-15:15 (closed Mondays)
Admission: 5 Yuan
Public Transport: Bus No. 810, 846, 2, 814, 819
Trolley Bus No. 103, 111

The Beijing Memorial Hall of the New Cultural Movement is found in the Red Building of Peking University (original site). The Memorial Hall comprehensively recounts the history of the New Cultural Movement with exhibits on the New Cultural Movement, reconstructed scenes, journals during the May 4th Movement in 1919, and videos. It is a vivid illustration of history starting from the birth of the New Cultural Move-

The Red Building of Peking University

The reading room where Mao Zedong once worked as a youth

ment to the establishment of the Chinese Communist Party, with over 90 photos and over 60 artifacts. The former office of Li Dazhao, then the director of the Peking University Library, has been reconstructed on the 1st floor. The reading room, in which Mao Zedong once worked, along with the big classroom where Peking University students had classes, have also been restored to their original appearance. In the exhibition hall for periodicals, over 20 types of journals and magazines, published during that period and preserved by the National Museum of China, are now on display. Two feature TV films, *The May 4th Movement* and *Former Residences of Luminaries in the New Cultural Movement*, made by the Memorial Hall of the New Cultural Movement, are regularly shown in the video room.

Beijing Police Museum

Location: 36 Dongjiao Minxiang Street, Dongcheng District
Telephone: 85222282, 85225018
Hours: 9:00-16:00 (closed Mondays)
Admission: 5 Yuan; students, free
Public Transport: Bus No. 9, 41, 60, 729, 744, 819, 859

The 2,000 sq. m exhibition space of the Beijing Police Museum displays the tremendous contributions and achievements made by the Beijing police in defending the stability and peace of public life in the capital city after New China was founded. The display presents the history of the People's Police primarily through objects, pictures, texts, models and videos. It

The exterior of the Beijing Police Museum

Wall relief in the lobby

Old rickshaw number plates

also offers such high-tech programs as virtual target practice, vehicle driving simulation, real-time road traffic display, and training for ordinary people on how to escape a fire.

Firefighting equipment in the old days

Yonghegong Lama Temple

Location: 12 Yonghegong Avenue, Dongcheng District
Telephone: 64044499, 64049027
Hours: 9:00-16:30
Admission: 25 Yuan; students, 12 Yuan
Public Transport: Bus No. 13, 62, 116, 117
Subway

Constructed in 1694, Yonghegong was the former residence of Emperor Yongzheng before he ascended the throne. It is also the largest Tibetan Buddhist monastery in the city of Beijing, as well as across China's mainland. The rich collection preserved in the temple includes great numbers of precious Buddhist statues, Thangkas (Tibetan scroll paintings), religious articles and vessels, as well as clothing, porce-

A gilt-bronze statue of Goddess Sgröl-ma

The Ten Thousand Happiness Pavilion (Wan Fo Ge) in Yonghegong Lama Temple

A gilt-bronze statue of Marici
(Goddess of Light)

lain and daily items used by different ethnic groups, all of great historical value. Various Buddhist statues and rare cultural relics are enshrined in the different halls of the temple. Among them are the "Mountain of Five Hundred Arhats" carved from red sandalwood, a shrine carved with *manmu* (Phoebe *nanmu*), and a Guinness-listed 18m-tall Buddha statue made from a single white sandalwood tree. Many of the exhibits preserved here were valuable gifts presented to the Qing imperial court and the lama temple by Tibetan aristocrats and eminent monks from the 16th century. These well-preserved items have exceptional historical as well as artistic value.

A copper statue of Baisajyagurvai

Confucius Temple and Imperial College

Location: 13 Guozijian Street, Dongcheng District
Telephone: 64042407, 64012118
Hours: 8:30-16:30
Admission: 10 Yuan; students, 3 Yuan
Public Transport: Bus No. 13, 44, 406, 820, 909
Trolley Bus No. 116
Subway

Both facing the south, the Confucius Temple and the Imperial College were built aligned with the former on the east side and the latter to the west, following the ancient Chinese custom of "temple on the left and college on the right." Here at the Confucius Temple in Beijing, people venerated Confucius through the Yuan, Ming and Qing dynasties. Its main architectural structures consisted of the Dacheng Gate, Dacheng Hall

The stone tablets bearing names of *jinshi* in the Yuan, Ming and Qing dynasties

The Dachong Gate and statue of Confucius

and the Sage Worship Hall. "Dacheng" implies that Confucius represents the compendium of Chinese culture. The Imperial College was once the highest administrative organ in charge of education and national learning institutions in ancient China. It was from here that many famous figures in Chinese history began their political careers from the Ming Dynasty onwards. The central building of the Imperial College is named Piyong, which is one of the "six great palaces" in Beijing, and the only ancient "school" remaining intact in the country today. Emperors used to come here to give lectures. The building now contains an exhibition on Confucius' life. The Imperial College has also preserved 190 valuable stone tablets engraved with *The Stele of Thirteen Classics,* as

Dacheng Hall

A musical performance held at a ceremony to venerate Confucius

well as 198 stone tablets bearing the names of *jinshi*, a title during the Yuan, Ming and Qing dynasties for those who passed the national exams.

The ancient classics that record the musical compositions used at ceremonies for venerating Confucius throughout history

The archway on Guozijian Street

National Wax Museum of China

Location: East side, Tiananmen Square, Dongcheng District
Telephone: 65128901
Hours: 8:30-16:30 (closed on the day before Spring Festival)
Admission: 20 Yuan; students, 10 Yuan
Public Transport: Bus No. 1, 2, 4, 5, 10, 20, 22, 37, 52; special bus route 1
Subway

The National Wax Museum is found inside the National Museum of China. As the largest and top state-level wax museum in China, it plans on displaying 300 to 400 wax figures over an exhibition floor space of several thousand square meters. The entire project was completed in 2007.

Tenmuji (Emperor Taizu of Yuan), founder of the Yuan

Zhang Heng, an ancient Chinese astronomer

The interior of an exhibition hall

Poly Art Museum

Location: 14 Dongzhimen Avenue S., Dongcheng District
Telephone: 65008117
Hours: 9:30-16:30 (closed Sundays)
Admission: 50 Yuan; students, 25 Yuan
Public Transport: Bus No. 44, 113, 115, 701, 800, 823
Trolley Bus No. 118
Subway

The Poly Art Museum was founded and financed by the China Poly Group Corporation in 1998. The establishment of the museum was based on the company's guidelines to promote the fine traditions of Chinese culture and art, to save and retrieve precious Chinese cultural relics scattered overseas, and promote enterprise culture. The museum is currently curating two special exhibitions. One is the Exhibition of Se-

An iron statue of the Bodhisattva

The Poly Building

lected Ancient Chinese Bronze Ware, displaying 150 pieces or sets of bronze objects from the period between the Shang and Tang dynasties. The other is the Exhibition of Selected Ancient Chinese Stone Carvings of Buddhist Images, including over 40 Buddhist stone carvings from the Northern Dynasty until the Tang Dynasty. The Poly Art Museum has been acclaimed as "one of the best modern museums in China today."

Square bronze vessel decorated with animal-mask motif

The zodiac statues originally from the Yuanmingyuan Garden, purchased back from overseas by Poly at a high cost

Beijing Museum for the Exchange of Cultural Relics

Location: 5 Lumichang Hutong (Alley), Dongcheng District
Telephone: 65250072, 65286691
Hours: 8:30-16:30 (closed Mondays)
Admission: 20 Yuan; students, 10 Yuan
Public Transport: Bus No. 24, 44, 750, 800, walk from the Lumichang stop

Located inside the Zhi Hua Temple, the Beijing Museum for the Exchange of Cultural Relics was converted from the former Zhihua Temple Cultural Relics Preservation Office in 1992. Its goal is to collect information and data about museums in Beijing, in China and even throughout the world, and to display the current conditions of all the museums in the Beijing region.

Zhihua Temple was built by Wang Zheng, a

The Pavilion of Ten Thousand Buddhas at Ru Lai Palace, Zhihua Temple

Ancient engraved plate of Buddhist scripts

Buddha Tathagata at the Zhihua Temple

Various types of precious scripts preserved in the temple

powerful eunuch in the Ming court, as his family temple, in the 8th year of Ming Emperor Zhengtong's reign (1443). Emperor Yingzong of the Ming Dynasty named it "Zhihua Zen Temple." Its rich collection of cultural relics now includes over 1,500 artifacts. The temple's large fresco about 4.8 m long and 3.1 m high, showing a scene of a sermon by the Kshitigarbha (Dizang) Buddha, is a priceless mural dated from the Ming Dynasty. *Lunzang* in the temple is the oldest of its type kept in Beijing. The "Jing Music" played at Zhihua Temple is one of the five great ancient musical genres in China. Having permeated 28 generations over 540 years, it is hailed as a "living fossil" in the field of music.

Ming-dynasty fresco at the Zhihua Temple

Beijing Ancient Observatory

Location: 2 Dongbiaobei Hutong, Jianguomen Gate, Dongcheng District
Telephone: 65242202, 65128923
Hours: 9:00-16:00 (closed Mondays)
Admission: 10 Yuan; students, 5 Yuan
Public Transport: Bus No. 1, 4, 9, 44, 48
Subway

The Beijing Ancient Observatory is situated at the southwestern corner of the Jianguomen overpass. As one of the oldest observatories in the world, it was built during the reign of Emperor Zhengtong of the Ming Dynasty (c. 1442). The ancient

The interior of the exhibition hall

observatory uninterruptedly conducted astronomical observation for 500 years, from 1422 to 1929, holding the longest record in history. It also enjoys great repute in the world for its well-preserved architecture and complete sets of equipment. The eight bronze astronomical instruments made in the Qing Dynasty are re-

Various ancient astronomical devices

A view of the Ancient Observatory from a distance

markable for their huge size, magnificent appearance and masterful sculpturing. Except for their traditional Chinese style in shape, ornamental design and workmanship, these astronomical instruments also reflect European developments and achievements in the manufacture of large astronomical instruments after the Renaissance. These huge instruments act as historical evidence of cultural exchange between East and West. Besides being actual equipment used for astronomical observation, they are also priceless artifacts unparalleled in the world.

Quadrant and a Chinese-style Armillary Sphere

Lao She Memorial Hall

Location: 19 Fengfu Hutong, Dengshikou Avenue W, Dongcheng District
Telephone: 65142612, 65599218
Hours: 9:00-17:00
Admission: 10 Yuan
Public Transport: Bus No. 2, 108, 814
Trolley Bus No. 103, 104

The Lao She Memorial Hall, former residence of Lao She, is an ordinary small courtyard locally known as *siheyuan* (traditional, residential compound with houses around a courtyard). The three rooms and two flanking chambers facing south have been kept intact, just as when Lao She and his fam-

A portrait of Lao She displayed in the center of the living room

lly lived here. The rooms in the east and west wings of the residence hold exhibits about Lao She's childhood and his literary career through six aspects, displaying a large number of the valuable books, photos, manuscripts and items that Lao She used during his lifetime. It has collected numerous versions and translations of

The former residence of Lao She – a standard Beijing-style *siheyuan* residence

Lao She's literary works from different periods. *Camel Xiang Zi* alone has more than 30 translations. The modest scope of the exhibition provides visitors a vivid review of the lifelong literary achievements of Lao She, impressing people with the unique charm of his works, and his lasting influence on younger generations.

An exhibition room

The Imperial City Art Museum

Location: 9 Changpu Riverside, Dongcheng District
Telephone: 85115114, 85115104
Hours: 9:00-14:30
Admission: 20 Yuan; students, 10 Yuan
Public Transport: Bus No. 1, 2, 4, 10, 20, 52, 59, 728, 802

The Imperial City Art Museum is the only place in Beijing that specializes in the study, excavation and display of ancient government buildings, temples, warehouses, gardens as well as imperial services including escorting and property management ritual ceremonies, as well as opera and entertainment in the capital city. Located inside Changpuhe Park on the east side of Tiananmen Gate, the museum is set in

A section of an exhibition hall

Porcelain ware preserved in the museum

Porcelain ware preserved in the museum

a Chinese *siheyuan* dwelling. Three exhibition halls and a multi-functional hall are arranged on two floors above and under ground. The basic exhibition in the museum is Flavors of the Imperial City, which vividly reveals the charm of the imperial city of Beijing through a variety of forms such as artifacts, pictures, models and texts.

Candlesticks from the Qing Dynasty

Former Residence of Mao Dun

Location: 13 Houyuan'ensi Hutong, Jiaodaokou Avenue S., Dongcheng District
Telephone: 64040520
Hours: 9:00-16:00
Admission: 5 Yuan
Public Transport: Bus No. 5, 13
Trolley Bus No. 104, 108

Originally named Shen Dehong, Mao Dun was born in the town of Wuzhen, Tongxiang, Zhejiang Province, in 1896. Influenced by the Soviet October Revolution, he committed himself to literary writing, choosing to use his pen to fight the cultural suppression of Kuomintang authoritarianism. He served as the head of the Chinese Ministry of Culture, vice-chairman of the National Committee of the Chinese People's Political Consultative Conference, vice-chair-

Courtyard in Mao Dun's former residence

Mao Dun's study

Mao Dun's manuscripts

man of the China Federation of Literature and Art Circles, as well as a long-time chairman of the Chinese Writers' Association.

The last residence of Mao Dun was a Beijing-style *siheyuan* dwelling where he spent his final years. The furniture in the house has been kept intact, just as when he lived here. The exhibition in the northern room introduces Mao Dun and his literary creation. The photos and objects displayed in the eastern wing shows the tireless contribution by Mao Dun to cultural development and world peace after New China was founded. The back section contains Mao Dun's study and bedroom.

Photos displayed concerning Mao Dun's life

Wen Tianxiang Memorial Hall

Location: 63 Fuxue Hutong, Dongcheng District
Telephone: 64014968
Hours: 9:00-17:00
Admission: 5 Yuan; students, 3 Yuan
Public Transport: Bus No. 2, 113
Trolley Bus No. 104, 108

Also known as the Memorial Hall of Prime Minister Wen, the Memorial Hall was built to commemorate Wen Tianxiang, a national hero and prime minister of the late Southern Song Dynasty (1127-1270). He led courageous resistance against the invasion of the Yuan. When the Yuan army invaded Southern Song territory in 1278, Wen Tianxiang led the resistance, fighting fearlessly until he was defeated and captured. Sent to the capital of the Yuan Empire at the time, he was imprisoned in an earthen

Wen Tianxiang Memorial Hall

cell in the Yuan-dynasty Ministry of Armies and Horses for four years. He remained unmoved in the face of the hard and soft tactics of the Yuan rulers. Preferring to die than to yield, in prison he wrote the immortal poem *Ode to the Moral Spirit.* The Memorial Hall built on the prison site preserves a number of valuable historical relics. These include the stone tablet inscribed with "The Biography of Song Prime Minister Wen," set up in the Ming Dynasty, the stone tablet erected in the Qing Dynasty for "Rebuilding the Monument," and the stone tablet of "Monument to Prime Minister Wen of the Song Dynasty." The Exhibition on the Life of Wen Tianxiang, on display in the Memorial Hall, provides a brief introduction to his lifelong heroic deeds. A folding screen standing in the exhibition hall has on its front side Mao Zedong's calligraphy of Wen's famous lines: "No one will be spared by death, yet a brave heart stays to serve the country." On the back is the complete text of Wen Tianxiang's poem *Ode to Moral Spirit.* A lush date tree in the Memorial Hall's back garden is said to have been planted by Wen himself when he was jailed here.

A section of the exhibition hall

The central hall

Wangfujing Palaeoanthropology Cultural Relics Museum

Location: WIP3, Oriental Plaza in Wangfujing, Dongcheng District
Telephone: 85186306, 85186307
Hours: 10:00-16:30
Admission: 10 Yuan; students, 5 Yuan
Public Transport: Bus No. 1, 4, 10, 52, 803, 814
Trolley Bus No. 103, 104

This site of palaeoanthropology relics was discovered at Wangfujing in 1996, when the Oriental Plaza was under construction. Buried 12 m below the ground and consisting of two layers of ancient culture in a gray-brown color, the relics belong to the late Old Stone Age, around 24,000 or 25,000 years ago. They demonstrate that ancient humans once inhabited the Wangfujing area, and may be the first discovery in the world of ancient human remains in the downtown of an international cosmopolis. Occupying an area of about 2,000 sq. m, over 2,000 cultural relics were unearthed from the site. The excavated stone and bone objects and the traces of fire usage have been maintained as they were first unearthed.

The lower jaw of an ancient ox unearthed from the site

The carcass of a Mongolian hare unearthed from the site

The ruins and the exhibition hall

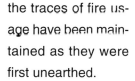

Beijing Museum of Tap Water

Location: A6 Courtyard, Dongzhimenwai Avenue N., Dongcheng District
Telephone: 64650787
Hours: 9:00-16:00 (closed Mondays & Tuesdays)
Admission: 5 Yuan; students, 2 Yuan
Public Transport: Bus No. 44, 117, 123, 800
Trolley Bus No. 106, 107
Subway

The exterior of the Beijing Museum of Tap Water

An old water-drawing apparatus used by Beijing residents in the past (replica)

As the first museum funded completely by the business sector, the Beijing Museum of Tap Water was opened to the public in 2000. Occupying a space of 1,500 sq. m, the museum was built on the original site of the Dongzhimen Water Plant, the first water plant built in Beijing, in 1908.

The museum offers a comprehensive display of the history of Beijing tap water over more than 90 years by using 130 real articles, 34 models and sand-tables, and 110 photographs. Using modern technology, it illustrates the complicated processes of making and distributing tap water throughout the city, the strict monitoring measures on water quality. Visitors learn how tap water is processed along with other useful knowledge.

Inside an exhibition hall

The Capital Museum

Location: 16 Fuxingmenwai Avenue, Xicheng District
Telephone: 63370491, 63370492
Hours: 9:00-17:00 (Ticket office closes at 16:00 every day; closed Mondays)
Admission: full price, 30 / 50 Yuan; half price: 15 / 25 Yuan
Public Transport: Bus No. 1, 4, 52, 37, 650, 45, 26, 727, 717, 937
Special bus route 1
Subway

The Capital Museum sits on the western extension of Chang'an Avenue – the famed premier street of China. Originally located in the Confucius Temple in Beijing, the museum was established in 1953. It was finally moved to the current address in May 2006.

The exhibitions housed in the Capital Museum are based on collections accumulated over the years and from antiques unearthed in the Beijing region. Through integrating the lat-

Blue-and-white Porcelain Pot with Phoenix Head, made in Jingdezhen

The exterior of the new Capital Museum

Inside an exhibition hall

est research results on the history, cultural heritage, archeological and other aspects of Beijing, the museum is famed for its modern and regional display on the city of Beijing. Its regular exhibitions include: Ancient Capital – Beijing's History and Culture, Ancient Capital – Beijing's Urban Construction, and Old Stories of Beijing – Display of Old Beijing Folk Customs. Its fine arts exhibitions include: Exhibition of Ancient Porcelain Masterpieces, Exhibition of Ancient Beijing Bronze Masterpieces, Exhibition of Fine Collection of Ancient Calligraphical Works, Exhibition of Collection of Ancient Paintings, Exhibition of Collection of Ancient Jade Ware, Exhibition of Collection of Ancient Buddha Statues, and Exhibition of Collection of Study Treasures. A total of 5,622 objects preserved in the museum are on display.

Beijing folk sculpture – "Carrying a Bridal Sedan"

Geological Museum of China

Location: Xisi, Xicheng District
Telephone: 66557858
Hours: 9:00-16:30 (closed Mondays)
Admission: 30 Yuan; students, 15 Yuan
Public Transport: Bus No. 13, 22, 38, 47, 68, 709, 726, 808, 826
Trolley Bus No. 101, 102, 103, 105, 109

Founded in 1916, the Geological Museum of China occupies an area of 11,000 sq. m, and mainly preserves collections of paleontological fossils, minerals, rocks and gems. Among its 200,000-odd pieces of various geological specimens, there are rare *Shantungosaurus giganteus* fossils, the largest cinnabar monocrystal ever found in the country, and the Yuanmou Man tooth fossil excavated in Yunnan Province – the earliest hominid fossil found to date in China. The museum also offers an introduction to all kinds of natural resources, the formation and evolution of the earth, as well as other topics.

A reproduced karst cavern

A silicon fossil

Inside an exhibition hall

China Palaeozoological Hall

Location: 142 Xizhimenwai Avenue, Xicheng District
Telephone: 88369210, 68935280
Hours: 9:00-16:30 (closed Mondays)
Admission: 20 Yuan; children and seniors, 10 Yuan
Public Transport: Bus No. 7, 15, 19, 27, 45, 332, 347
Trolley Bus No. 102, 103, 107, 111

Fossil of a Chinese fish with wolf fins – from the Late Jurassic Age about 140 million years ago

The exterior of the China Palaeozoological Hall

The China Palaeozoological Hall is a museum that specializes in the natural sciences. The museum houses more than 200,000 fossil samples of vertebrates of various kinds from various regions of China. The displays are organized into the Vertebrates Hall and Shuhua Palaeohuman Hall, which follow the stages of palaeozoological evolution. The Vertebrates Hall is further divided into the Ancient Fish Hall, the Ancient Amphibians Hall, the Ancient Reptiles

and Birds Hall, as well as the Ancient Mammal Hall. The "fish" fossils from several billion years ago, the huge skeletons of dinosaurs and Yellow River mastodons are all part of this rare and invaluable collection of the museum.

Fossils of the Mamenxi Hechuan dinosaur and Qingdao dinosaur

Temple of Ancient Monarchs

Location: 131 Fuchengmennei Avenue, Xicheng District
Telephone: 66120186
Hours: 8:30-16:30
Admission: 20 Yuan; students and seniors, 10 Yuan
Public Transport: Bus No. 13, 42, 709, 814, 823, 850
Trolley Bus No. 101, 102, 103

Originally constructed in the 9th year of the reign of Emperor Jiajing during the Ming Dynasty (1530), the Temple of Ancient Monarchs is the only royal family temple remaining in China today, where royal ceremonies were held to worship the Three Emperors and Five Sovereigns of ancient times, as well as the later emperors and meritorious civil and military subjects. The main building of the temple, Jingde Chongsheng Hall, retains the architec-

Jingde Chongsheng Hall – Ming architecture preserved in the Temple of Ancient Monarchs

tural style of the Ming Dynasty. This is where the Three Emperors and Five Sovereigns of ancient China were venerated. Now it houses the memorial tablets for 188 people including emperors in Chinese history. Today the temple also offers displays such as, "Main Figures Worshipped in the Temple of Ancient Monarchs," "Development of the Temple of Ancient Monarchs," "Three Emperors and Five Sovereigns and 100 Chinese Surnames," and "The Culture of Lord Guan Worship."

Exhibition of the main figures venerated in the temple

A section of the memorial tablets for the emperors in Jingde Chongsheng Hall

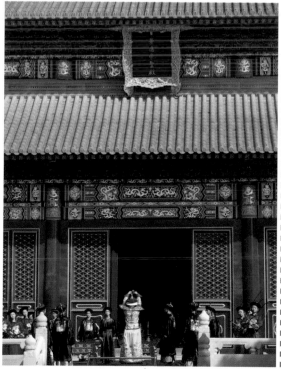

A memorial ritual by the Qing emperors replicated in the Temple of Ancient Monarchs

Beijing Planetarium

Location: 138 Xizhimenwai Avenue, Xicheng District
Telephone: 68352453, 68312570
Hours: Wednesday-Friday: 10:00-16:00; Saturday-Sunday: 9:00-16:30
(closed Mondays & Tuesdays)
Admission: 15 Yuan
Public Transport: Bus No. 7, 15, 19, 27, 45, 332, 334, 347, 708, 814, 104,
105, 106
Trolley Bus No. 102, 103, 107, 111

As a national museum specializing in the natural sciences, the Beijing Planetarium focuses on dissemination and education about astronomy for the public, through the reproduction of a starry night sky, displays of astronomy knowledge, and sessions for space observation.

The Planetarium consists of the old and the new planetariums. Opened to the public in 1957 and covering an area of about 7,000 sq. m, the

The Planetarium – a popular science educational base for youngsters in Beijing

old planetarium has an optical projector, exhibition hall, assembly hall, and an observatory. The new planetarium houses a digital space theater, 3D space simulator and 4D projection hall. It is also equipped with a lab for solar observation, a public observatory and a classroom for the teaching of astronomy.

An iron meteorite

National Arts and Crafts Museum

Location: 101 Fuxingmennei Avenue, Dongcheng District
Telephone: 66053476
Hours: 9:30-16:30 (closed Mondays)
Admission: 8 Yuan; students, 4 Yuan
Public Transport: Bus No. 1, 4, 10, 15, 52, 57, 802
Special bus route 1
Subway

A night view of the National Arts and Crafts Museum

A large jade sculpture

The National Arts and Crafts Museum specializes in the collection and presentation of modern state-level treasures in the country. Covering an area of 1,800 sq. m, the museum houses four exhibition halls, basically displaying cloisonné ware, artistic porcelain, drawnwork and embroidery, inside-bottle painting, artistic lacquer, as well as other folk arts and crafts. Among its collections are several precious artworks that have won national and international top awards, along with some masterpieces by the finest artists and artisans in China.

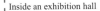

Inside an exhibition hall

China Currency Museum

Location: 22 Xijiao Minxiang Street, Xicheng District
Telephone: 66058326, 66081385
Hours: 9:00-16:00 (closed Mondays)
Admission: 10 Yuan; students, 5 Yuan
Public Transport: Bus No. 5, 22, 44, 48, 59, 66, 120, 819, 922

This is a national museum specializing in the collection and study of currencies. Covering an area of 1,800 sq. m, the museum houses five sections for displaying the history of Chinese currency: the Unification of Chinese Currencies, Round Heaven and Square Earth, Gold and Silver Coins, Banks and Banknotes, and the Present and the Future. The museum also preserves a large number of Chinese and foreign currencies, as well as related artifacts.

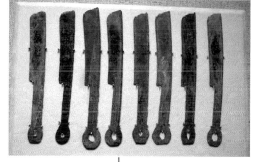

Ancient coins in straight knife shapes

Ancient gold coins

A money house in modern Chinese history (a replica)

Kuaixue Hall Calligraphy Museum

Location: Northern section of Beihai Park, Xicheng District
Telephone: 64062278
Hours: 9:00-16:15
Admission: Free with park admission
Public Transport: Bus No. 5, 101, 812, 814, 846
Trolley Bus No. 103, 109, 111

The Kuaixue Hall Calligraphy Museum is located inside Kuaixue Hall in Beihai Park. The museum displays calligraphic works and stone inscriptions by famous calligraphers throughout various dynasties in China. It also demonstrates the ancient processes of producing China's "four treasures of the study," i.e., writing brush, ink-stick, ink-slab and paper. The most famous exhibits in the museum are a page from *Kuaixue Shiqing* (Swift Snow Turned Clear), written by Wang Xizhi (303-361); and "Note on Kuaixue Hall," written by Emperor Qianlong of the Qing

The corridor with inscribed stone slabs

Dynasty (1644-1911).

The *Kuaixue Hall Stone Inscriptions* are mounted on the wall inside the east-west corridors of Kuaixue Hall. According to historical records, the authentic writing of Wang Xizhi, a renowned calligrapher in the Jin Dynasty (265-420), was obtained by Feng Quan, a great scholar of the late Ming Dynasty (1368-1644).

"Happiness" character, written by Emperor Qianlong

Feng Quan selected a further 80 calligraphic works of 20 famous calligraphers from the Jin to Yuan dynasties, to make up his selection of 81 calligraphic masterpieces. Feng asked Liu Guangyang, a well-known contemporary engraver, to engrave the 81 pieces onto stone slabs – hence the invaluable *Kuaixue Hall Stone Inscriptions*. By the 44th year of the Qianlong reign in the Qing Dynasty (1779), Yang Jingsu,

Kuaixue Hall, built with *nanmu*

the governor-general of Fujian and Zhejiang, bought these stone inscriptions for an exorbitant price, and dedicated them to Emperor Qianlong. Greatly excited, Qianlong ordered the addition of a quadrangle behind the Yulan Pavilion on the northern shore of Beihai Lake, and the building of a large *nanmu* (*Phoebe nanmu*) hall, naming it Kuaixue Hall, to preserve these priceless treasures. He ordered the stone slabs to be set into the walls of the corridors along the east and west wings of the hall. Emperor

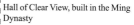

Hall of Clear View, built in the Ming Dynasty

Qianlong also specially composed an essay entitled "Note on Kuaixue Hall," and had it inscribed onto a stone slab, setting this into the corridor wall too. He wrote a poem to honor the event: "Now that the remaining 'Swift Snow Calligraphy' is displayed for the world, our past heritage leads to today, as we now meet ancient friends."

The Exhibition Hall of China's Cultural Palace of Ethnic Groups

Location: 49 Fuxingmennei Avenue, Xicheng District
Telephone: 66016806 , 66024433 (ex. 5238)
Hours: 9:00-16:30
Public Transport: Bus No. 1, 4, 7, 10, 15, 37, 38
Subway

A Mongolian singer performing a long Mongolian song at "The Exhibition on Achievements of the Protection of the Intangible Cultural Heritage"

The first "Exhibition on Human Rights in China," inaugurated at the Exhibition Hall of China's Cultural Palace of Ethnic Groups

Exhibition Hall of China's Cultural Palace of Ethnic Groups

Located on West Chang'an Avenue in Beijing, the Exhibition Hall of China's Cultural Palace of Ethnic Groups was one of the top ten architectural sites built for the 10th anniversary of the birth of the People's Republic of China. Once hailed as the No. 1 premier palace of New China by the British book *World Architectural History*, the building was selected as "one of the masterpieces of architectural art in modern China" by the Second Convention of the International Association of Architects in 1999. It was also voted as the winner of the 50 most favorite architectural structures by the Chinese public, during the activity of "Our Most Loved Traditional Chinese Architecture" poll held in Beijing in 1994.

The Exhibition Hall of China's Cultural Palace of Ethnic Groups sets its objectives on the collection and preservation of the cultural relics of China's ethnic minorities, as well as the studying and advocacy of the cultures of ethnic minorities. With an exhibition area of more than over 3,000 sq. m., the Hall displays more than 40,000 cultural items. It also hosts exhibitions on special topics from time to time.

Beijing Exhibition Hall of Ancient Currencies

Location: Inside the embrasure watchtower of Deshengmen Gate, North 2nd Ring Road Central, Xicheng District
Telephone: 62018073
Hours: 9:00-16:00 (closed Mondays)
Admission: 10 Yuan; students, 5 Yuan
Public Transport: Bus No. 5, 27, 44, 55, 305, 315, 345, 380, 815, 819, 919 Subway

The Beijing Exhibition Hall of Ancient Currencies is situated inside the 500-year-old embrasure watchtower of Deshengmen Gate. Opened to the public in 1993, it has preserved nearly 1,000 pieces of coins and other currencies from various Chinese dynasties. Ranging from the "shell money" used in the Shang Dynasty (1600-1046 BC), through to the paper "Zhiyuan Common Notes" during the Northern Song Dynasty (960-1127), to the copper coins in of the Republic of China, every piece of currency on display here reveals each era's political and economic conditions and the level of development in Chinese history. Short-term exhibitions on specific topics are also held here. It is an ideal place for hobbyists to study and exchange ideas about their collections.

The silver ingot circulated during the Xianfeng reign of the Qing Dynasty

Knife coins

The Beijing Exhibition Hall of Ancient Currencies in the embrasure watchtower of the Deshengmen Gate

Former Residence of Guo Moruo

Location: 18 Qianhai Xijie Street, Xicheng District
Telephone: 66125392 , 66125984 , 66182789
Hours: 9:00-16:30 (closed Mondays)
Admission: 20 Yuan; students, 10 Yuan
Public Transport: Bus No. 13, 42, 107, 111, 118, 701, 810, 823, 850

Statue of Guo Moruo in the courtyard

Guo Moruo's former residence is a large-scale *siheyuan* occupying an area of 7,000 sq. m. It had once been the site of horse stables of Prince Gong's residential palace during the Qing Dynasty. Guo Moruo (1892-1978) spent the last 15 years of his life here, and many of his valuable manuscripts, books and cultural relics have been kept here. The gingko trees and peonies that Guo Moruo and his wife planted are still blossoming in the courtyard. In the spacious *siheyuan*, a mound of earth right behind the entrance is dotted with trees. In the second section of the *siheyuan*, the five northern rooms were once Guo's study and sitting room. The east chamber was his bedroom, and there are three rooms each on the east and the west flanks. All the rooms are connected by a long corridor leading to the backyard. "The Exhibition of Guo Moruo's Life" here revives his unusual life experience as a poet, a scholar and a fighter. Visitors are impressed with Guo Moruo's simple life style and his romantic temperament as a poet and a revolutionary at the same time.

The former residence of Guo Moruo

Former Residence of Soong Ching Ling

Location: 46 Northern Riverside Street, Houhai, Xicheng District
Telephone: 64073653
Hours: 9:00-16:00
Admission: 20 Yuan; students, 10 Yuan
Public Transport: Bus No. 5, 305, 734, 815

The former residence of Soong Ching Ling (1893-1981), wife of Dr. Sun Yatsen, was once the garden of Prince Chun's mansion in the Qing Dynasty. Soong lived here from 1963 until she died, on May 29th 1981. The main architecture in the courtyard is a small two-storey

The courtyard with a statue of Soong Ching Ling

building. The exhibition in the building displays nearly 400 pictures of Soong Ching Ling's life, and over 300 pieces of cultural artifacts. The interior of the building in the middle courtyard is arranged as it was when Soong lived here. On the first floor, a portrait of Dr. Sun Yatsen was hung on the east wall of the small drawing room. On the second floor are her bedroom, living room and study. Still lying on the desk in her bedroom are some books she used to read, documents, and a pair of reading glasses. By the shores of Houhai Lake stands a dove shelter. This former residence is not only an elegant and pleasant spot for sightseeing, but also the best place for visitors to remember the noble spirit of Soong Ching Ling.

The waiting room in the former residence of Song Ching Ling

Lu Xun Museum

Location: 19 Fuchengmennei Avenue, 2th alleyway, Gongmenkou, Xicheng District
Telephone: 66156548 , 66156551
Hours: 9:00-16:00 (closed Mondays)
Admission: 10 Yuan; students, 5 Yuan
Public Transport: Bus No. 13, 42, 709, 814, 823, 850
Trolley Bus No. 102, 103
Subway

A bust of Lu Xun

The Lu Xun Museum opened to the public on the 20th anniversary of Lu Xun's death on 19 October 1956 is the earliest "Memorial Hall for Literary Masters," set up after New China was founded. A new exhibition hall housed in a Beijing-style *siheyuan* was added next door to the former residence in 1994.

The Lu Xun Museum has collected more than 30,000 cultural artifacts, including Lu Xun's manuscripts, books and letters, diaries, as well as his collections of books, an ancient brick relief dated from the Han Dynasty, and epitaph rubbings. "The Life of Lu Xun," the key exhibition held here, provides a vivid and comprehen-

The Lu Xun Museum

A room added to the north room at the former residence was used as Lu Xun's bedroom and study; many of Lu Xun's masterpieces were written in this room, which was also nick-named "Tiger's Tail."

sive illustration of the glorious life of Lu Xun, who has been hailed as the "commander-in-chief of China's revolution in culture."

The former residence of Lu Xun is a small elegant quadrangle. It has three rooms each on the north and south side, with one chamber each on the east and west side. Things have been retained as when Lu Xun lived there, especially the small room of only around 8 sq. m, attached to the central north room, which served both as his bedroom and study.

The former residence of Lu Xun to the west of the Museum

Memorial Hall of Guo Shoujing

Location: A60 West Avenue, Deshengmen Gate, Xicheng District
Telephone: 66183083
Hours: 8:30-11:30, 13:30-17:00
Admission: 0.5 Yuan
Public Transport: Bus No. 22, 27, 44
Subway

Guo Shoujing (1231-1316) was originally from Shunde Xingtai (today's Xingtai, Hebei Province). He was a renowned astronomer, a water conservancy scientist, a mathematician and an instrument craftsman of the Yuan Dynasty. He made great contributions to the cause of water conservancy in China's history. He directed projects that harnessed the waters of over 100 rivers and lakes in China. For example, his direction of projects such as "Diverting water from Yuquan Spring," "Opening up water resources in Dadu and building the Baifuyan Dam," and "Digging through the

Memorial Hall of Guo Shoujing

62

A bust of Guo Shoujing

Tonghui River," not only solved the problem of locating water resources for Dadu, capital of the Yuan Empire, but also helped transform Dadu into a prosperous shipping center. At the same time, in order to calculate and design an accurate calendar, he invented more than 20 astronomical instruments, including the simplified armilla, scaphe, armillary sphere, and a direction-determining compass. He joined in the design of the "time-service calendar," similar to the modern Gregorian calendar, except that its formulation was over 300 years earlier than the European invention.

The Memorial Hall of Guo Shoujing consists of three halls exhibiting his great achievements.

The interior of an exhibition hall

Mei Lanfang Memorial Museum

Location: 9 Huguosi Street, Xicheng District
Telephone: 66180351
Hours: 9:00-11:30, 13:00-16:00
Admission: 10 Yuan; students, 5 Yuan
Public Transport: Bus No. 55, 22, 38, 47, 409, 709, 726, from the Huguosi stop, walk east; Bus No. 13, 42, Trolley Bus No. 107, 111, 118, from the Changqiao stop, walk north.

A bust of Mei Lanfang

His ancestral home in Taizhou, Jiangsu Province, Mei Lanfang (1894-1961) was one of the four famous masters playing female characters in Beijing opera. After Mei Lanfang passed away in 1961, a memorial museum was founded for him on a proposal by Premier Zhou Enlai. The front yard of his former residence was converted into an exhibition area, displaying his artistic career through a great number of pictures and artifacts. The three north rooms in the back garden were kept intact, just as when Mei lived there. The hardwood furniture, the pier-glass mirror he used for practicing, the dove whistle, and the other small items Mei Lanfang used throughout his lifetime, are all kept in the

The courtyard of the former residence of Mei Lanfang

The opera costumes once worn by Mei Lanfang

waiting room. A painting entitled *The Thirteen Best Performers during the Reigns of Tongzhi and Guangxu*, by Shen Rongpu, a Qing-dynasty artist, is hung on the west wall of the room. The inner chamber, connecting to the waiting room, served as the living room. Mei Lanfang's study in the west wing has been converted into an exhibition room of his achievements, and his bedroom in the east wing is now a small video theatre showcasing Mei's superb performances.

Mei Lanfang's bedroom in the former residence

Xu Beihong Museum

Location: 53 Xinjiekou Avene N., Xicheng District
Telephone: 62252042, 62276936
Hours: 9:00-16:00 (closed Mondays)
Admission: 5 Yuan; students, 2 Yuan
Public Transport: Bus No. 22, 27, 38, 44, 47, 726, 810
Subway

A statue of Xu Beihong

Born in Yixing, Jiangsu Province, Xu Beihong (1895-1953) was one of China's most renowned artists and fine-arts educators. The museum was relocated in 1983, from Xu Beihong's former residence to the present address, after the former residence was demolished due to subway construction. Covering 2,700 sq. m, the museum preserves over 1,200 artworks by Xu Beihong, as well as over 10,000 books and paintings collected by Xu through his lifetime. The paintings *Jiu Fanggao and His Steed, Tian Heng's 500 Heros, The Foolish Old Man Moves Mountains*, and others among the collection, are rare masterpieces in China's modern art history.

An exhibition hall

China Agricultural Museum

Address: 16 East 3rd Ring Road, Chaoyang District
Telephone: 65096068, 65931355
Hours: 9:00-16:00 (closed Mondays)
Admission: 10 Yuan; students, free
Public Transport: Bus No. 43, 115, 117, 302, 300, 402, 405

Located in the National Agricultural Exhibition Hall, the China Agricultural Museum, occupying an area of 10,000 sq. m, is the only museum specializing in Chinese agriculture. The rich collection of the museum includes more than 1,000 specimens under various categories. It holds permanent exhibitions such as "The Scientific and Technical History of Ancient Chinese Agriculture," "The Aquatic Products of China," and "The Agricultural Resources of China." Both informative and interesting, these exhibitions illustrate the history of agricultural civilization in China over the past several thousand years.

Inside an exhibition hall

Inside an exhibition hall

National Agricultural Exhibition Hall

China Science and Technology Museum

Location: 1 North 3rd Ring Road Central, Chaoyang District
Telephone: 62371177 (ex 2109)
Hours: 9:00-16:30 (closed Mondays)
Admission: 30 Yuan; students, 20 Yuan
Public Transport: Bus No. 300, 302, 367, 387, 407, 409, 702, 718, 725, 801, 825

A chameleon

A robot orchestra conductor

China Science and Technology Museum is the largest and most comprehensive museum on science and technology in the nation. It is consisted of Exhibition of Ancient Chinese Inventions, Hall of Mathematics, Physics and Chemistry, Hall of the Earth's Environment, Hall of Life and Hall of Engineering. It also houses labs for experiments in physics, chemistry, biology, electronics, computers, earth sciences, astronomy, and model building. There is also a large Astro-vision cinema plus a rich collection of scientific books in the museum.

The exterior of the China Science and Technology Museum

Museum of China's Ethnic Groups

Location: 1 Minzuyuan Road, Chaoyang District
Telephone: 62063647
Hours: 8:30-18:00
Admission: 60 Yuan for one park; 90 Yuan for both parks
Public Transport: Bus No. 21, 407, 737, 740, 819, 849, 941, 944, 951

Also known as the Chinese Cultural Park of Ethnic Groups, the Museum of China's Ethnic Groups is a large cultural base covering various ethnic minorities in China, including their traditional buildings, customs, songs and dances, handicrafts, as well as food and delicacies.

Spread over about 45 hectares, the museum is divided into the North Park and the South Park. The former contains 16 villages of the Tibetan, Miao, Ni, Hezhe and other peoples in an area of 20 hectares. The latter contains 21 scenic spots depicting regions inhabited by different peoples of Xinjiang, Inner Mongolia, Yunnan, and other places. The main building of the museum is located here as well. All the architectural structures in the two parks were built on a 1:1 proportion with the actual buildings, and reproduce the cultural heritage of the various peoples of China. The museum holds festival celebrations every month. Visitors can enjoy and participate in the singing and dancing, festivities, productive activities, games, handicraft making and other events, as they explore the two parks of the museum.

A Miao stilt-house (replica)

69

The Chinese Cultural Park of Ethnic Groups

Beijing Museum of Aeronautic and Astronautic Models

Location: Heiqiao Village, Nangao Township at Dashanzi, Chaoyang District
Telephone: 64372990
Hours: 8:30-17:30
Admission: 20 Yuan; students, 10 Yuan
Public Transport: Bus No. 403 or 813, get off at the Huantie stop; Bus No. 402 or 418, walk from the Nangao stop

A model of an MIG-15 81S attack aircraft

The Beijing Museum of Aeronautic and Astronautic Models is the first model museum in China. With a total acreage of 26,000 sq. m, the museum consists of a "small airport" – a launch pad for air, naval and land models – an exhibition hall, a workshop, a teaching lab, and other facilities. The museum integrates hands-on participation, knowledge learning, military training and scientific education, turning it into an ideal large classroom involving visitors in viewing, creating and training activities of astronavigation and aviation.

Various plane models displayed in the exhibition hall

China Sports Museum

Location: A3 Andingmen Road, Chaoyang District
Telephone: 64912167
Hours: 8:30-16:30
Admission: 5 Yuan
Public Transport: Bus No. 18, 108, 803, 328, 358, 387

The China Sports Museum is situated south-east of the National Olympics Center and has an exhibition area of 2,510 sq. m. The displays in the museum are divided into: Ancient Chinese Sports, Modern Chinese Sports, General Fitness Sports, and Olympic Sports. Using a large number of artifacts, photographs and models, these exhibitions illustrate the glorious progress of China's athletic activities through the ages. Especially fascinating displays are those on Chinese martial arts, *qigong* (breathing exercises), polo, *Jiaodi* (sumo) and *Cuju* ball (football), all reflecting distinctive traditional Chinese characteristics as well as ancient Chinese sports culture.

Ming-dynasty porcelain bowl painted with children

China Sports Museum

China Railway Museum

Location: East of North Jiuxianqiao, east of the railroad loop, Chaoyang District
Telephone: 51836872
Hours: 9:00-16:00 (closed Mondays)
Admission: 20 Yuan; student groups, free
Public Transport: Bus No. 403

An old steam locomotive made in Great Britain

The interior of an exhibition hall of the museum

A state-level comprehensive museum covering the railway system of China, the museum displays a collection of more than 60 valuable locomotives and carriages. Among the large collection of 30 steam locomotives are the renowned "No. 0 Locomotive," the "Mao Zedong Locomotive" and the "Zhu De locomotive," full of general historical and revolutionary significance. There are also locomotive models such as the JF, KD7, SN, SL and KF that represent every stage of the splendid history of over a century of railway construction in China. The museum has also carefully preserved the first editions of the "Victory," "Construction," "People," "Advance" and other series of locomotive models made in China after 1949.

The "Mao Zedong" steam locomotive

National Museum of Modern Chinese Literature

Location: 45 Wenxueguan Road, Chaoyang District
Telephone: 84619071, 84619060
Hours: 9:00-16:30
Admission: 20 Yuan; students, 10 Yuan
Public Transport: Bus No. 119, 409, 422

The National Museum of Modern Chinese Literature was opened to the public at its new location in May 2000. The new site houses 52 libraries with a total collection of over 300,000 items including books, letters, manuscripts, photographs and other cultural artifacts left by a great number of modern Chinese writers. There are four exhibition halls in the museum: "Exhibition of 20th Century Chinese Literary Masters," "Exhibition of Modern Chinese Literature," "Contemporary Chinese Literature" and "Writers' Libraries." Equipped with an up-to-date internet connection, the museum at its new location is one of the largest comprehensive literary museums in the world.

Statues of Ye Shengtao, Lao She and Cao Yu – great masters of modern Chinese literature, in the courtyard of the museum

A section of an exhibition hall

National Museum of Modern Chinese Literature

China Film Museum

Location: 9 Nanying Road, Chaoyang District
Telephone: 64319548, 64349100, 64346100
Hours: 9:00-16:30 (closed Mondays)
Admission: 20 Yuan; students, 10 Yuan
Public Transport: Bus No. 402, 418, 813, 909, 973, walk from the Nangang stop

A scene of film making

The newly opened China Film Museum

The China Film Museum was opened to the public on February 10, 2007. Covering an area of 37,930 sq. m, it is the largest museum in the world dedicated to motion pictures.

The museum houses a total of 20 exhibition halls. The permanent exhibitions held in the museum display more than 1,500 films, 4,300 photographs, as well as textual introductions to over 450 film industry workers. The museum is equipped with an IMAX theater, a digital theatre, and three 35mm film projection rooms. The IMAX theatre in the museum is distinctive, possessing the best imaging system in the world, the largest screen in Asia, and a state-of-the-art 6-track sound system. It has gained praise for taking audiences through "the ultimate experience in film viewing."

China Red Sandalwood Museum

Location: 9 Xinglong Street W., Gaobeidian, Chaoyang District
Telephone: 85752818, 85752822
Hours: 9:00-17:00
Admission: 50 Yuan
Public Transport: Bus No. 312, 728
Subway

Opened to the public in September 1999, the China Red Sandalwood Museum has an exhibition space of 9,569 sq. m. It is the largest museum specializing in the collection of red sandalwood works in China today, resulting from the generous commitment of Ms. Chen Lihua, a member of the National Committee of the Chinese People's Political Consultative Conference.

Traditional Chinese hardwood furniture

The exterior of the China Red Sandalwood Museum

A traditional Chinese screen engraved with dragons

The museum itself is a work of art in the tradition of Chinese architecture. The five stories of the museum's building display wooden sculptures in red sandalwood, ebony, rosewood, and *nanmu*, alongside several hundred pieces of traditional furniture dated to the Ming and Qing dynasties.

A replica of the emperor's throne preserved in the Hall of Heavenly Purity of the Forbidden City

The Art Gallery of the Central Academy of Fine Arts

Location: 8 Huajiadi Street S., Chaoyang District (inside the Chinese Central Academy of Fine Arts)
Telephone: 64771123
Hours: 9:00-16:00
Admission: 5 Yuan
Public Transport: Bus No. 701, 710, 420

Built in 1960, the art gallery is a specialized art museum under the Central Academy of Fine Arts. It focuses on the systematic collection of various types of artworks for the purpose of education and exhibition. The gallery has preserved famous paintings by ancient, modern and contemporary artists in China. Besides temporary exhibitions of ancient Chinese paintings and oil paintings from its collection, the gallery also organizes special art displays for members of the Central Academy of Fine Arts, as well as the general public, with works from international art exhibitions and others.

Opened to the public in October 2007, the new gallery covers a space of 14,777 sq. m, and consists of two stories underground and four stories aboveground.

An exhibition of outstanding works by graduate students in its general hall

The art gallery at its old location at the Central Academy of Fine Arts on Wangfujing

Traditional Chinese Medicine Museum

Location: 11 East 3rd Ring Road, northern end of Heping Street, Chaoyang District
Telephone: 64286679, 64286835
Hours: 8:30-11:30, 1:30-4:30 (Tuesdays & Fridays only)
Admission: 10 Yuan; students, 5 Yuan
Public Transport: Bus No. 13, 62, 119, 300, 302, 367, 407

The exterior of the Traditional Chinese Medicine Museum

An edge roller used to grind herbs

An exhibition hall

Located inside the Beijing University of Traditional Chinese Medicine, the museum specializes in traditional Chinese medicine and herbs. It is divided into two sections, one focusing on herb samples from traditional Chinese medicine, and the other on the history of traditional Chinese medicine. The two sections occupy an area of 2,300 sq. m. The section on the history of traditional Chinese medicine preserves valuable cultural artifacts, rare books, portraits and statues, as well as achievements made in this and related fields. The section on traditional herb samples displays materials and ingredients found in Chinese herbal medicine, as well as all types of herbal samples.

Jintai Art Museum

Location: West gate, Chaoyang Park, 1 Nongzhanguan Rd. S., Chaoyang District
Telephone: 65019441
Hours: 9:30-16:30
Admission: With park admission
Public Transport: Bus No. 302, 710, 805

The Jintai Art Museum was built with funds donated by a group of famous artists and calligraphers. The primary feature of this art museum is its collection of more than 100 portraits and statues of political VIPs and cultural celebrities from around the world, as created by Yuan Xikun, the curator of the museum. Focusing on its collection of famous artworks and calligraphy from various Chinese dynasties, the museum also holds research and exchange activities about Chinese painting and traditional Chinese art, and has recently emerged as an ideal venue for artists to display their works as well as to discuss culture and art.

A statue of Mahatma Gandhi

A bust of Ferdinand de Magellan

A bust of Zygmunt Y. Padlewski

A section of an exhibition hall

Yan-Huang Art Gallery

Location: 9 Huizhong Road, Yayuncun, Chaoyang District
Telephone: 64912902
Hours: 9:00-16:30 (closed Mondays)
Admission: 5 Yuan; students, 3 Yuan
Public Transport: Bus No. 108, 328, 358, 387, 803

The exhibition hall of contemporary artworks

The Yan-Huang Art Gallery is a large modern art gallery sponsored by the celebrated Chinese artist Huang Zhou, and built with donations from the Chinese public and government. Its mission is to collect and display outstanding national works of art, and to provide a space for artistic exchanges between Chinese and international artists and collectors. The art gallery focuses on the preservation of

The exterior of the Yan-Huang Art Gallery

Children Playing in a Courtyard in Autumn, by Su Hanchen in the Song Dynasty (painting detail)

contemporary and ancient Chinese paintings, calligraphy and cultural artifacts. In recent years it has already collected several hundred pieces of painted pottery, pottery figurines and folk artworks.

The exhibition hall of traditional Chinese paintings

Beijing Folklore Museum

Location: 141 Chaoyangmenwai Avenue, Chaoyang District
Telephone: 65510151, 65514148
Hours: 8:30-16:30 (closed Mondays)
Admission Fee: 10 Yuan; students, 5 Yuan
Public Transport: Bus No. 110, 112, 420, 750, 813, 846, 858
Trolley Bus No. 101, 109
Subway

A big brass urn, popular everyday ware for Beijing folks of old

The exterior of Dongyue Temple

The Beijing Folklore Museum is located inside Dongyue Temple, a cultural site comprised of ancient buildings from the Yuan, Ming and Qing dynasties, listed as one of the Historical Monuments and Cultural Relics under State Protection. Established in 1997, the museum aims to protect and research the cultural history of Dongyue Temple, to research the folklore of the Beijing region, and to study, display and advocate the fine cultural traditions of Chi-

nese people. As the largest Taoist temple of the Zhengyi branch in north China, Dongyue Temple was the site of national ceremonies for centuries. The folk fair held regularly at Dongyue Temple is also the earliest and largest of its type in Beijing region. A great number of inscribed stone tablets kept in the temple are an important historical record for the research in folk beliefs and social structures. Among the stone tablets collected by the temple, the *Monument of Taoist Virtue*, written by Zhao Mengfu, a renowned calligraphic work of the Yuan Dynasty, possesses extremely important artistic and historic value. The temple holds an all-year-round exhibition on old Beijing life, etiquette and customs. It also hosts a vibrant folk celebration during traditional festivals such as Spring Festival, the Dragon Boat Festival, the Mid-Autumn Festival and the Double Ninth Festival.

God and Goddess for Posterity, worshipped in the Guangsi Hall at Dongyue Temple, are supposed to bless worshippers with "bountiful children and happiness."

A stone roller

A bronze "Te," a supernatural beast with a horse's head, mule's body, donkey's tail and ox's hooves, said to be Emperor Wenchang's mount

Guanfu Museum

Location: 18 Jinnan Road, Dashanzi, Chaoyang District
Telephone: 64338887
Hours: 9:00-17:00
Admission: 20 Yuan; students, 10 Yuan
Public Transport: Bus No. 418, 813, 909, get off at the Zhangwanfen stop

The exterior of the Guanfu Museum

The Guanfu Museum was opened to the public on January 18, 1997. With its collection focusing on rare cultural artifacts from the Ming and Qing dynasties, the museum has mainly preserved ceramics, ancient furniture and craftwork. Its exhibition halls are decorated with

Furniture Hall – the Rosewood Furniture Room

The Hall of Ceramics

elegance and simplicity, conveying to visitors the attractive flavor of traditional Chinese residences. Accompanied by the charming music of ancient Chinese harps, visitors are allowed to touch and enjoy the exhibits here. All of this conjures a unique ambience and style for this museum.

A plate-mouth vase decorated with peony designs, made in the Dangyangyu Kiln during the Northern Song Dynasty

A celadon bowl, carved through and decorated with a depiction of "Enjoying a Peaceful Springtime Forever," made during the Wanli Reign of the Ming Dynasty

Furniture Hall – the Mahogany Furniture Room

Beijing Museum of Natural History

Location: 126 Tianqiao Avenue S., Chongwen District
Telephone: 67023096, 67024431
Hours: 8:30-18:00
Admission: 30 Yuan; students, 15 Yuan
Public Transport: Bus No. 2, 17, 20, 25, 35, 110
Trolley Bus No. 105, 106

The Beijing Museum of Natural History is the first large museum of natural history in the country. Among the 200,000 or so specimens preserved in the museum, many are listed as first- and second-class animals and plants under national protection. It also possesses a certain number of specimens and rare samples of particular significance. Specimens include fossils of a Yellow River Mammoth, a 26m-long Malong Creek Mammoth and a Chinese Santa bird – one of the earliest kinds of birds on earth – and an entire nest of dinosaur eggs, the only

Skeleton of the Yellow River Mammoth

The Ancient Reptile Hall – Dinosaur Room

one extant of its kind. The museum hosts four large permanent exhibitions: "The Ancient Animal Exhibition" (divided into the Ancient Reptile Hall, Ancient Mammal Hall, Hall of the Origin of Creatures and Early Evolution, and Hall of Thriving Invertebrates), "The Botanical Exhibition", "The Animal Exhibition" (Including the Hall of Animals – Friends of Humans, and Hall of Mystery of Animals), and "The Exhibition of Humans". The four exhibitions constitute a panorama on the origin and evolution of life on Earth. Following the main line of evolution of creatures, the exhibition's goal is to display the colorful varieties of creatures and popularize life-science knowledge. There are also special displays in the museum, including "The Wonder of a Human Body," "Aquatic Creatures" and "The Dinosaur World." Furthermore, the popular science center of the museum – the "Exploration Corner" – offers interactive exploration of natural mysteries to curious young visitors.

The exterior of the Beijing Museum of Natural History

Museum of a Hundred Kinds of Crafts

Location: B12 Guangming Road, Chongwen District
Telephone: 67126612, 67131673
Hours: 9:00-17:00
Admission: Free
Public Transport: Bus No. 6, 8, 35, 41, 60, 116, 705, 707

Craft-making on site

The term "hundred kinds of crafts" originated in the official book *On Crafts*, written in the Qi Kingdom during the Spring and Autumn and Warring States periods (770-221 BC). Each dynasty, Yuan, Ming or Qing, had its own governmental department to manage the production of art and craft for the royal palace. This imperial department was known among the people of the time as "Hundred Kinds of Crafts." The Museum of a Hundred Kinds of Crafts is where the production, display and sale of traditional Chinese handicrafts are gathered in one locale. Here, visitors enjoy breathtaking performances of "masters" from every trade in handicrafts. "Experience firsthand superb skills, and study all the remarkable details."

The exterior of the Museum of a Hundred Kinds of Crafts

Display of embroidery

Beijing Mumingtang Ancient Porcelain Museum

Location: 1 Central Huashi Beili, Chongwen District
Telephone: 67186939, 67187266
Hours: 10:00-18:00
Admission: 10 Yuan
Public Transport: Bus No. 23, 40, 43, 48, 57, 610, 715

The Beijing Mumingtang Ancient Porcelain Museum has preserved about 50,000 pieces of porcelain ware, divided into 30 categories, and dated according to successive dynasties and periods. Its collection is primarily characterized by its ancient porcelain and pottery work made in several major official and individual kilns from the Tang and Song dynasties onward. Its large collection of porcelain ware by the Ru Kiln, from the Song Dynasty, is particularly impressive. Visitors can touch and appreciate the exhibits in the special "hands-on area" in the museum.

The porcelain relic, "A Deer Looking Back"

Beijing Muming Tang Ancient Porcelain Museum

Beijing Museum of Ancient Architecture

Location: 21 Dongjing Road, Xuanwu District
Telephone: 63172150, 63172151
Hours: 9:00-16:00
Admission: 15 Yuan; students, 8 Yuan
Public Transport: Bus No. 7, 15, 17, 20, 36, 54, 120, 729, 742, 859

The Beijing Museum of Ancient Architecture is a museum specializing in the research and display of China's ancient architectural history, culture and technology. The museum introduces the development of Chinese ancient architecture from the preliminary forms through to the highest accomplishments during the Ming and Qing dynasties, with a large number of photographs, elaborate models and artifacts.

The caisson in an architectural model from the Ming Dynasty

A model of the Tong ethnic group's "wind and rain building"

Among the exhibits, the model of old Beijing is hailed as the No. 1 sand-table work in the country. The caisson artwork of the "Longfu Temple Caisson in Beijing" is the only one remaining in the country. The model of the "Hall of Prayer for Good Harvests in the Temple of Heaven," along with other architectural replicas, illustrates the unique charm of the ancient architectural structures of China.

The Gate of the Xiannong Altar

Museum of Chinese Buddhist Books and Relics

Location: 7 Front Street, Fayuan Temple, Xuanwu District
Telephone: 63533772
Hours: 8:30-11:00, 13:30-16:00 (closed Wednesdays)
Admission: 5 Yuan
Public Transport: Bus No. 6, 19, 50, 53, 61, 109

The Museum of Chinese Buddhist Books and Relics lies inside the Fayuan Temple, which has a long history of 1,300 years. Founded in 1980, the Museum specializes in the collection, exhibition and study of Buddhist relics and books. The exhibition housed in the Museum is divided in two sections: "Display of Different Editions of Buddhist Scriptures through the Ages" and "Display of Buddhist Statues through Different Dynasties." The most precious artifacts

Various Buddhist statues preserved in the Relics Hall of Chinese Buddhist Books

94

preserved here include scriptures handwritten in the Tang Dynasty and the Five Dynasties, incomplete and damaged Buddhist scriptures from the Song and the Yuan dynasties and a wood carving of a

Stone-inscribed scriptures dating from different ages

7.4m-long statue of a reclined Buddha from the Ming Dynasty.

One of four bronze deva kings, dating from the 15th century

The theater in the museum

Beijing Museum of Traditional Opera

Location: 3 Hufang Road, Xuanwu District
Telephone: 63518284, 63529134
Hours: 9:00-19:30
Admission: 10 Yuan; students, 5 Yuan
Public Transport: Bus No. 6, 14, 15, 23, 25, 45, 66
Trolley Bus No. 102, 105

A section of an exhibition hall

Costumes used by masters of traditional opera

The Museum of Traditional Opera combines several roles into one, as a theatre for opera performances, a museum for exhibition, and an institute for research on the heritage and cultural relics of opera in the country. It was established in 1994 at the former site of the Hu-Guang Guild Hall in Beijing. With its extensive historical and cultural displays, it has bore witness to a vast plethora of talent and cultural elegance. Tan Xinpei, Yu Shuyan, Mei Lanfang and other masters of Peking opera all performed on its stage. The Hu-Guang Guild Hall was listed as a protected cultural site by the Beijing government in 1984.

The gate tower of the Beijing Museum of Traditional Opera

China Stamp Museum

Location: Building No. 2, Xuanwumen Avenue E., Xuanwu District
Telephone: 65185511
Hours: exhibitions on specific topics from time to time; pre-booking required
Public Transport: Bus No. 14, 15, 22, 44, 45, 48

The China Stamp Museum is situated in the building of the China National Philatelic Corporation at Hepingmen. It houses an exhibition area of 5,000 sq. m and has collected 200,000 types of Chinese and foreign stamps. Its stamp exhibits are divided into four categories: "Stamps of the Qing Dynasty and the Republic of China," "Stamps of the National Revolutionary War Period," "Stamps and Their Records, Original Designs and Copies, and Famous Works in New China," and "Taiwan Stamps and Stamps of Countries in the Universal Postal Union."

One Yuan small-font stamp of the Qing Dynasty, preserved in the museum

"Stamp Exhibition on World Aviation and Astronavigation," held at the museum

Visitors at a stamp exhibition

Songtangzhai Folk Carving Museum

Location: 1 Liulichang Street E., Xuanwu District, Beijing
Telephone: 83164662
Hours: 9:00-18:00 (closed every other Monday)
Admission: 20 Yuan; students, 10 Yuan
Public Transport: Bus No. 7, 14, 15, 25, 44, 848
Subway

A gate tower with carved bricks from Shanxi Province

The Songtangzhai Folk Carving Museum

Carved ornaments on traditional Chinese folk dwellings

Situated at the eastern end of Liulichang Street, the Songtangzhai Folk Carving Museum is privately owned by a collector – Li Songtang. The site used to be the Zhongyong Book Bureau of the Ming and Qing dynasties, and the Yimin Bookstore during the Republic of China era. Covering a space of 254 sq. m, it is one of the few well-preserved old stores in Beijing. It has collected over 1,000 objects, ranging from ancient bricks of the Qin Dynasty (221-206 BC), as well as tiles from the Han (206 BC-220), and stone, wood and brick carvings, folk architectural artifacts and ornaments, and household knickknacks, along with furniture from the Ming and Qing dynasties. The most precious items among these are the eave tiles, with ends carved with designs of double-fish from the early Spring and Autumn Period, as well as an extant gate bearing from Dadu, capital of the Yuan Dynasty.

Beijing Red Mansions Culture and Art Museum

Location: Nancaiyuan Street, Xuanwu District
Telephone: 63544994, 63544993
Hours: 8:30-16:30
Admission: 15 Yuan; students, 8 Yuan
Public Transport: Bus No. 10, 19, 56, 59, 61, 122, 423, 819
Special bus route 3

The museum is a replica of the splendid classical garden of the aristocratic family immortalized in the classic Chinese novel *A Dream of Red Mansions*, authored by Cao Xueqin. It is also the main location where the TV series *A Dream of Red Mansions* was shot. Built in 1984 and fully opened to the public in 1989, the museum covers an area of 13 hectares. Besides elegant

Yihong Garden

The Honghan Biyin Pavilion and its long corridor winding through the park

pavilions and kiosks surrounded by scenic ponds and small hills, the museum also presents a display of Red Mansion Culture and Art, a folkways performance, and the large water show "The Illusion of Red Mansions."

Molded figures of characters from the novel *A Dream of Red Mansions*

Museum of Ancient Pottery Civilization

Location: 12 Youanmennei Avenue W., Xuanwu District
Telephone: 63538811, 63538884
Hours: 9:00-17:00 (closed Mondays)
Admission: 20 Yuan; students, 10 Yuan
Public Transport: Bus No. 10, 19, 56, 59, 61, 122, 423, 819

As one of the first set of privately owned museums to emerge in the country, the Museum of Ancient Pottery Civilization is the first to specialize in pottery ware. Its collection includes over 2,000 unearthed relics that belong to major categories of painted pottery from the Neolithic Age, pottery relics from the Zhou, Qin, Han and Tang dynasties, eave tile ends from the Warring States Period, and clay seals from the Qin and Han dynasties. With ancient pot-

The Museum of Ancient Pottery Civilization

Painted pottery

tery civilization as its primary focus and aesthetic archeology as its key feature, the museum offers a comprehensive and vivid display of the ancient pottery civilization of China, presenting a systematic demonstration of the manufacture, utilization and aesthetics of the pottery ware of ancient Chinese civilization.

Many of the exhibits at the museum are rare, being the only such relics found by archeologists in China so far. In particular, the clay seals from the Qin Dynasty constitute another very important discovery in the field of Qin Dynasty cultural study. They may be regarded as the first set of the "Chart of Officials" and "Map of Geographical Locations" from a unified feudal dynasty in Chinese history, and an initial record of the ancient Chinese political system. The basic exhibition of the museum is in four parts, with 600 exhibits: Ancient and Painted Pottery, Ends of Eave Tiles, Clay Seals, and Ancient Pottery. Aimed at combining public education, art appreciation and professional research at the same time, the exhibition presents the public with the lasting and unique charm of the civilization of ancient pottery.

The interior of an exhibition hall

Xuan Nan Culture Museum

Location: 9 Changchun Street, Xuanwu District
Telephone: 83167249
Hours: 9:00-16:00 (closed Mondays)
Admission: Free
Public Transport: Bus No. 477, 348, 10, 6, 822, 109, 717

The Xuan Nan Culture Museum lies inside Changchun Temple in the southern part of the city of Beijing. Focusing on the display of the folk culture of Xuan Nan (southern Xuanwu District) in Beijing, the museum vividly exhibits the long history and rich cultural heritage of Xuan Nan. The museum houses eight exhibition halls, including "The Long History of Xuan Nan," "Footprints of Heroes," "A Century's Com-

A replica of Ruifuxiang Silk Store – a famous shop of Beijing

Sculptures – traditional trades in old Beijing

mercial Prosperity," "Flourishing Peking Opera," and "Paradise of Southern Beijing." Visitors will witness the rich and colorful folk culture as well as the modern facets of the southern Xuanwu District in Beijing. The museum, departing from the traditional division of artifacts, photographs and texts, presents an innovative arrangement in its exhibits.

The main exhibition hall

Former Residence of Ji Xiaolan

Location: 241 Zhushikou Avenue W., Xuanwu District
Telephone: 63037636 (ex-105)
Hours: 9:00-16:00
Admission: 6 Yuan
Public Transport: Bus No. 743, 715, 57
Trolley Bus No. 105

The former residence of Ji Xiaolan is found on the north side of Zhushikou Avenue W., where the Jinyang Restaurant is located. The residence's "Yuewei Cottage" is a traditional Chinese *sihoyuan*, or quadrangle, in two sections. One chamber in the residence is shaped like a boat, and once a horizontal plate, inscribed with "Boat by the Bank," was hung above its door. Another chamber resembles a connecting corridor, and a horizontal plate inscribed with "Yuewei Cottage" was once hung inside it. The pea vine (wisteria) growing in the front courtyard and the cherry-apple tree in the rear courtyard, from Ji Xiaolan's lifetime, still remain. A lush ancient locust tree shades the front gate. Flowers bloom colorfully and fragrantly here every April and May.

The gate tower, modeled in a Western architectural style.

The Former Residence of Ji Xiaolan

China People's Revolution Military Museum

Location: 9 Fuxing Road, Haidian District
Telephone: 66866244
Hours: 8:30-17:30
Admission: Free
Public Transport: Bus No. 1, 4, 21, 52, 57, 320, 337
Subway

The site of the "Zunyi Meeting" (replica)

The exterior of the People's Revolution Military Museum

Founded in 1959, the China People's Revolution Military Museum covers an area of 60,000 sq. m. It is the only comprehensive museum in the country specializing in the military profession. The museum has preserved 120,000 historical artifacts, displayed in two open squares and a dozen exhibition halls. Among them, the main

exhibition halls are "The Second Revolutionary Civil War," "The War of Resistance against Japanese Aggression," "The Third Revolutionary Civil War," "Safeguarding Socialist Revolution and Construction," "Weaponry," and "Ancient and Modern Wars." They illustrate and highlight the military history and culture of China over 5,000 years. The content and form of the exhibitions are impressively diverse and colorful, imbued with the national characteristics of China.

Exhibition commemorating the 70th anniversary of the Long March carried out by the Red Army

The pistol used by Marshall Nie Rongzhen during the Long March

Scene of "the Red Army wading through marshy grassland."

The World Art Museum of the China Millennium Monument

Location: A9 Fuxing Road, Haidian District
Telephone: 68527108, 68513322
Hours: 9:00-18:00 (closes at 17:30 in the winter)
Admission: 30 Yuan (additional fees for special shows)
Public Transport: Bus No. 1, 4, 32, 57, 65, 320, 337, 414, 728, 827
Special bus routes 1, 5, 6
Subway

An American Indian priestess with outstretched arms

The China Millennium Monument where the World Art Museum is located was built to celebrate the millennium on the eve of the 21st century. Occupying an area of 350,000 sq. m, the architecture includes a turning "Qian" (heaven) facade and a solid "Kun" (earth) basis. The diameter of the round "Qian" surface is 47 meters. The solid "Kun" structure houses a circular corridor for exhibitions, and is now hosting a two-year-long exhibition entitled "The

The "Last Days of Bombay Exhibition," held at the China Millennium Monument

The fresco "Millennium Ode to China," done in rock relief in the round Millennium Hall

An Egyptian mortuary figure

Great Civilizations of the World." Valuable exhibits from 14 famous European and American museums display the 5,000-year-old civilizations of Mesopotamia, Egypt, India, the Americas, Greece and the Roman Empire. The round Millennium Hall in the museum is decorated with a large magnificent fresco made with a multicolor rock relief mural, entitled "Millennium Ode to China."

Inside the World Civilization Exhibition

Vishnu Sleeping on an Endless Snake, from India

The Ancient Bell Museum in the Big Bell Temple

Location: A31 West 3rd Ring Road, Haidian District
Telephone: 62550819, 62641384
Hours: 8:30-16:30
Admission: 10 Yuan; students, 4 Yuan
Public Transport: Bus No. 302, 367, 379, 422, 425, 718, 727, 730, 836, 967

The Ancient Bell Museum is located in the famous Big Bell Temple in Beijing. Originally built in the 11th year of the Yongzheng reign of the Qing Dynasty (1733), the temple was locally referred to as the "Big Bell Temple," as it houses a giant Buddhist bell cast during the Yongle reign of the Ming Dynasty. The museum has a fairly complete collection of over 400 ancient bells of various kinds, including musical bells, court bells, Buddhist bells, Taoist bells and Vajira bells. The most precious bell among these is the Giant Yongle Bell. Cast in 1420 and hailed

The entrance to the Big Bell Temple

112

The Yongle Bell from the Ming Dynasty

The interior of an exhibition hall

A Buddhist bell from the Yuan Dynasty

as the "king of bells with five absolutes," the bell is 6.75 m high, 3.3 m in diameter, and weighs about 46.5 tons. There are over 100 types of Buddhist sutras in Chinese and Sanskrit languages neatly inscribed on entire surfaces inside and outside the bell. With altogether 227,000 characters, these sutra texts make it the bell with the most inscribed words in the world. Its clear and pleasant ringing may be heard 40 to 50 km away. The Ancient Bell Museum is the only one of its kind in China, featuring the collection, exhibition, study and exploration of the value of ancient bells and their textual bearings, as well as disseminating knowledge about ancient bells to the public. Besides the basic display of various ancient bells, the museum also holds all types of activities to offer visitors consultation, research and exchanges on ancient bells.

Beijing Aviation Museum

Location: 37 Xueyuan Road, Haidian District, Beijing
Telephone: 82317512, 82317513
Hours: 8:30-12:00, 14:00-17:00 (closed Mondays)
Admission Fee: 4 Yuan; students, 2 Yuan
Public Transport: Bus No. 331, 375, 386, 392, 398, 706, 902

Located on the campus of the University of Aeronautics and Astronautics of Beijing, this is the first aviation museum in China opened to the public. Founded in 1986, the museum occupies an area of 9,700 sq. m and displays more than 30 aircraft models of various types from different historical periods. The planes on display include the famous P-61 Model Black Widow, the P-47 Model Lightning, the GRMK Sparrow Hawk, and the Beijing No. 1 Plane. Also on display are a large number of aircraft models, photographs and videos showing the history of aviation, the progress of aviation in China, and space exploration. Other exhibits include light and su-per-light aircrafts, jet and piston aviation engines, plane gauges, and parts of combat aircrafts. It is an ideal place for aviation fans to update their knowl-edge.

The exterior of the Beijing Aviation Museum

A D-61 night fighter

Inside an exhibition hall

Beijing Museum of Stone Carving Art

Location: 24 Wutasi Village, Baishiqiao, Haidian District
Telephone: 62186081, 62173543
Hours: 9:00-16:00 (closed Mondays)
Admission: 20 Yuan; students, 10 Yuan
Public Transport: Bus No. 320, 332, 347, 601, 717, 727, 808, 827, 904
Trolley Bus No. 105

Sculpted figures along a tomb passage

Inscribed tablets from various dynasties, collected from around the Beijing region

The Beijing Museum of Stone Carving Art focuses on the display of fine stone carvings found in the Beijing region. Occupying an area of 20,000 sq. m, the museum is in the Zhenjue Temple of former times, built during the Yongle reign of the Ming Dynasty. A Vajira-throne Pagoda in the museum, with its body fully covered with sculpted Buddha images, dates to the 9th year of the Chenghua reign (1473). One of a dozen similar pagodas remaining in China today, this pagoda with its greater age compared to others and its rather unique structure, is an important historical relic and a large rare

ancient work of art.

The indoor exhibition in the museum consists of the "Display about Zhenjue Temple," "Human and Stone – A Brief History of Stone Carving," and "Stone Artworks in the Beijing Region." The outdoor exhibition of the museum, entitled "Outdoor Display of Stone Carvings," displays stone inscriptions and carvings, tablets of merit, tablets of epitaphs, rubbings from stone inscriptions, temple and guildhall tablets. They exemplify the outstanding stone artworks of the Beijing region. The museum also possesses a rare stone tablet from the 1st year of the Yuanxing reign during the Eastern Han Dynasty (AD 105), known as the "No. 1 Carved Stone in Beijing." Another highly valued stone tablet, with a Bojinghui portrait from the Northern Song Dynasty, is believed to recount the evolution of stone carving. A third stone tablet with a carved chart of acupuncture points, from the Song Dynasty, is of extremely high scientific value. You can also see the stone railing panel from Dadu, capital of the Yuan Dynasty, representing the fashion in carving of Yuan times, and several pieces of elegantly carved stone monuments dated to the Qing Dynasty.

Sculpture of the Taihe reign of the Northern Wei Dynasty (499 AD)

Stone monument for a prince in the Qing Dynasty

Vajira-throne Pagoda, built in 1473

Museum of Ethnic Groups, Central University for Nationalities

Location: 27, Zhongguancun Avenue S., Haidian District
Telephone: 68932760
Hours: 8:30-11:30, 14:00-17:00
Admission: 10 Yuan; students, 5 Yuan
Public Transport: Bus No. 320, 332, 717, 727, 827, 808, 105, 106
Special bus routes 4, 6

Exhibition hall

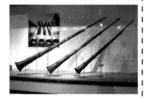

A brass horn

The Museum of Ethnic Groups, located on the campus of the Central University for Nationalities, preserves more than 20,000 articles that belong to 14 categories of cultural artifacts. These include classical texts, costumes, production tools and historical relics. Visitors are able to gain a systematic and profound learning experience regarding all of China's ethnic groups, and particularly its minorities. They can see the simple ancient bark clothing of the Hani people, the fish-skin clothing of the Hoche people, and the elegant Buddha statues and Thangkas of the Tibetans. The exhibits in the museum reward visitors with revelations that fill the eye.

The exterior

Beijing Art Museum

Location: Inside Wanshou Temple, West 3rd Ring Road N., Haidian District
Telephone: 68413380, 68413379
Hours: 9:00-16:00 (closed Mondays)
Admission: 20 Yuan; university students, 10 Yuan; primary & middle-school students, free
Public Transport: Bus No. 300, 323, 374, 730, 811, 817, 830, 831

The Beijing Art Museum is located in the Wanshou Temple (Temple of Longevity) of the Ming and Qing dynasties. The Wanshou Temple was built during the Wanli reign of the Ming Dynasty (1577), as a royal family temple. Renovated several times by emperors Kangxi, Qianlong and Guangxu in the Qing Dynasty, it gradually became an important site that combined the functions of a temple, the emperor's temporary dwelling and a garden for his family. It was once known as the "small forbidden city in west Beijing."

The exterior of the Wanshou Temple

A gilt-bronze statue of Buddha Variocana in the Grand Hall of the temple

Founded in 1985, the Beijing Art Museum houses about 50,000 ancient art objects of diverse categories. The rich and wide-ranging collection here mainly includes calligraphy, paintings and tablet inscription rubbings from the different dynasties, as well as manuscripts by eminent figures, palace embroidery, porcelain ware, ancient furniture, coins from various ages, and seals and stamps. The museum has also preserved over 100,000 copies of classical books published from the Song Dynasty (960-1279) onwards, until the Republic of China (1912-1949) period. Besides the ancient Chinese artworks, there are also a number of foreign artworks, and masterpieces by great artists such as Qi Baishi, Zhang Daqian and Xu Beihong. Seven permanent exhibitions are now held in the museum: "Historical Changes of Wanshou Temple", "Display of Seal Cutting," "Display of Buddhist Artworks," "Display of Ming and Qing Craft," "Display of Ming and Qing Porcelain," "Display of Fine Arts," and "Display of Ming and Qing Furniture."

Inside the Porcelain Exhibition Hall

Wenchang Gallery in the Summer Palace

Location: Summer Palace, Summer Palace Road, Haidian District
Telephone: 62881144
Hours: Summer: 8:30-17:00; Winter: 9:00-16:30
Admission: 20 Yuan
Public Transport: Bus No. 330, 332, 333, 346, 362, 375, 375 (sub-route), 384, 394, 801, 808, 904

The gate tower of Wenchang Gallery

Perched on the northeast side of Wenchang Pavilion in the Summer Palace, the Wenchang Gallery occupies an area of 5,660 sq. m and was opened to the public from September 1, 2000. It is the largest of China's top-class cultural museums set midst a classical land-scaped garden. The gallery has preserved more than 40,000 cultural artifacts from as early as the Shang and Zhou dynasties until the late Qing Dynasty. Many of its exhibits are rare relics of high value.

Rare bronzeware preserved in the Wenchang Gallery

A portion of an exhibition hall

An exhibition hall with antique decoration

China Museum of Telecommunications

Location: 42 Xueyuan Road, Haidian District
Telephone: 62303662, 62303627
Hours: 9:00-16:00 (closed Mondays)
Admission: 10 Yuan; students, 5 Yuan
Public Transport: Bus No. 331, 375, 386, 392, 398, 703, 719, 902

The China Museum of Telecommunications is an all-inclusive museum specializing in displays on the history and culture of Chinese communications, as well as on China's scientific and technological achievements in the realm of telecommunications. The museum occupies an area of 7,000 sq. m and houses three exhibition halls: the General Hall, the Telecommunications History Hall, and the Popular Science Hall. The exhibits illuminate the evolution of telecommunications in China over the past several thousand years, from ancient beacon towers and postal stations to modern postal traffic, and new scientific advances in mobile, digital, multimedia and ATM technologies.

The interior of the Museum of Telecommunications

A manual switchboard used in the late Qing Dynasty

A post office in the Qing Dynasty (replica)

大清郵政分局

Exhibition Center of Yuanmingyuan Ruins Park

Location: Inside Yuanmingyuan Ruins Park, Qinghua Road W., Haidian District
Telephone: 62568872
Hours: 7:00-19:00
Admission: Free with park admission
Public Transport: Bus No. 331, 375 (sub-route), 716, 717, 810, 814 Special bus route 6

A section of the exhibition hall

The Exhibition Center of the Yuanmingyuan Ruins Park was founded in 1979. With a great number of precious cultural relics, photographs and videos, and a miniature replica of the original three sections of Yuanmingyuan (also known as the Old Summer Palace), it presents a detailed introduction to the landscapes of Yuanmingyuan, and reproduces the world-famous garden in its glory days.

The painting *A Peacock Displays Its Tail Plumes*, by Guiseppe Castiglione; the two peacocks depicted in the painting were once reared in the park.

The ruins of the Western-style building (Sea Viewing Pavilion) in Yuanmingyuan

Midsummer in Yuanmingyuan

Sackler Museum of Art and Archeology in Peking University

Location: On Peking University campus, Haidian District
Telephone: 62751668, 62759784
Hours: 9:00-16:30
Admission: 5 Yuan
Public Transport: Bus No. 332, 716, 717, 718, 726, 732, 106

Pottery jars

The Sackler Museum of Art and Archeology in Peking University

The Sackler Museum of Art and Archeology is located at Minghe Garden in Peking University. Opened to the public in May 1993, the museum was jointly built by Dr. Arthur Sackler of the US, a friend of the Chinese people and Peking University. As a university museum specializing in archeology, the museum has preserved tens of thousands of items. The majority of its collection is made up of the special specimens collected from archeological work conducted in China at different times. The specimens include the stone tools used by the Peking Hominid found at the ruins of Zhoukoudian, items representing the archeological discoveries of the Neolithic Age, inscribed oracle bones from the Shang Dynasty, and bronze and jade ware excavated from a Western Zhou tomb in Qu Village, Shanxi Province. There are also relics of pottery, coins, clay seals, and other cultural folk relics. Besides the frequent exhibitions of relics collected by the Archeology Department of Peking University for the purpose of teaching and research, the museum has also organized temporary displays of major discoveries in the field, and exchanges exhibitions with related museums and universities.

The Bee Museum of China

Location: Inside Fragrant Hill Botanical Garden, Haidian District
Telephone: 82590094, 82594910
Hours: 8:00-16:00 (closed November 15–March 15)
Admission: 2 Yuan
Public Transport: Bus No. 318, 331, 360, 733, 833, 904

The Bee Museum of China occupies 150 sq. m and is located inside the Fragrant Hill Botanical Garden. Using actual objects, photographs and specimens, the museum displays everything about bees, including their origins and evolution, the history of apiculture and its resources in China, the biology of the bee, as well as apicultural techniques and products. The museum also offers consultations on bee-related products and human health.

A huge bee comb found in Xishuangbanna, Yunnan Province

The Bee Museum of China, in the Botanical Garden in Beijing's western suburbs

The Tomb of Li Dazhao

Location: Wan'an Cemetery, Hanhe Road, Haidian District
Telephone: 62591044
Hours: 8:30-11:00, 13:00-15:00
Admission: Free
Public Transport: Bus No. 331, 360, 714, 733, 833

A section of the exhibition room

Li Dazhao, one of the founders of the Communist Party of China (CPC), made pioneering contributions to the progress of China by launching the New Culture Movement, establishing the CPC, as well as supporting the early cooperation between CPC and Kuomintang. Killed by a reactionary warlord in 1927, Li Dazhao was buried at the Wan'an Cemetery by members of the underground CPC in 1933.

An upright statue of Li Dazhao, sculpted in white marble, stands at the entrance of the tomb. Behind the statue are the tombs of Li Dazhao and his spouse, Zhao Renlan. Behind the tombs is a monument with an epitaph written on the front by Deng Xiaoping, and an epitaph by the Central Committee of the CPC at the back.

The statue of Martyr Li Dazhao in the cemetery

The exhibition room on the west side of the courtyard displays "The Revolutionary Deeds of Martyr Li Dazhao," introducing his heroic life and immortal achievements.

Cao Xueqin Memorial Hall

Location: Inside the Fragrant Hill Botanical Garden
Telephone: 62591561 (ex-2028)
Hours: 8:30-16:30
Admission: Free with park admission to the Garden
Public Transport: Bus No. 331, 318, 360, 733, 904, 112

Cao Xueqin moved to Xishan (Western Hills) in Beijing's suburbs in the last years of his life and started writing his famed novel there. A number of experts believe that this old-style folk dwelling, with several poems written on the walls of a room which were found in 1971, located in

A traditional Chinese folk residence waiting room, in the museum

Zhengbaiqi Village in the area of the Fragrant Hill, was where Cao Xueqin wrote his immortal novel *A Dream of Red Mansions*. Based on their findings, a memorial hall was established at the location — a quadrangle encircled by low walls. The Qing architectural-style front and back wings have a total of 18 rooms. The exhibition rooms in the front display the living environment of the Manchu people in the Qing Dynasty, some models of Cao Xueqin's life and writing experiences in the Western Hills, as well as the major discoveries about Cao Xueqin made over the past two centuries. There are also special books and articles on Cao Xueqin and a room called "Wind Resisting Pavilion." This is the room where Cao Xueqin's handwriting was discovered on the wall. The six rooms in the back wing display the family background of Cao Xueqin, the influences on his immortal novel *A Dream of Red Mansions*, as well as his other works.

The ancient well in the courtyard of the Cao Xueqin Memorial Hall

Display Hall of Quaternary Glacier Striations

Location: 28 Moshikou, Shijingshan District
Telephone: 88720993, 88722585
Hours: 9:00-17:00
Admission: 5 Yuan
Public Transport: Bus No. 311 or 336, walk east from the Shougang Residential Quarters stop

The Display Hall of Quaternary Glacier Striations was jointly founded by the Chinese Ministry of Geology and Mineral Resources along with several other organizations in 1987, at the site where the striations, or long scratches, of the Quaternary Glacier were discovered. Verified by the renowned geologist Li Siguang, the site has first such striations found in northern China. The Display Hall offers a rich exhibition of geological fossils, photographs and charts of China's geological and topographical conditions.

The interior of the Display Hall

The site of the Quaternary glacial striations

The exterior of the Display Hall

Beijing Eunuch Cultural Museum

Location: 80 Moshikou Avenue, Shijingshan District
Telephone: 88724148
Hours: 9:00-16:00
Admission: 8 Yuan; students, 4 Yuan
Public Transport: Bus No. 331, 336, 396, 959, 746, 337, 354

Exhibition hall

Located west on Moshikou Avenue in Shijingshan District, the Beijing Eunuch Cultural Museum is at the cemetery of Tian Yi, a powerful Ming-dynasty eunuch in charge of the royal seal. Built in 1605, the cemetery faces south and consists of the Virtue Display Hall, the Longevity Section, and the Convent of Compassion. Encircled by a stone wall, the cemetery occupies 6,000 sq. m and contains five tombs of Tian Yi and other eunuchs. Constructed mainly with stone carvings and sculptures, the cemetery is known for its high standards, exquisite carving and rich content. Large and completely preserved, it remains the only top-level eunuch cemetery in the country. Also, it is the only museum in China today specializing in eunuch culture.

Stone figures in front of the tomb of Tian Yi

The Memorial Hall of the Chinese People's War of Resistance against Japanese Aggression

Location: 101 Chengnei Street, Wanping, Fengtai District
Telephone: 83892355
Hours: Summer: 8:00-17:00; Winter: 8:30-16:30
Admission: Free
Public Transport: Bus No. 309 (sub-route), 339, 709, 715, 964, 971, 983

The Memorial Hall of the Chinese People's War of Resistance against Japanese Aggression was built by the Lugou Bridge inside Wanping Town. It consists of the exhibition section and a semi-panorama art gallery. The former has "The Hall of National War against Japanese Invasion," "The Hall of the People's War," and "The Hall of Anti-Japa-

A crater left from the July 7th Incident

The exterior of the Memorial Hall of the Chinese People's War of Resistance against Japanese Aggression

Replica of the scene when Japanese invaders surrendered in Nanjing

nese Heroes." The semi-panorama art gallery displays a huge oil-painting spanning 180 degrees. Utilizing modern audio-visual technologies, it vividly relives the historic scenes of the "July 7th Lugouqiao Incident." The extensive historical materials, photographs and objects in the memorial hall present an objective historical record for the public.

Sculpture of heroes

China Space Museum

Location: 1 Dahongmen Road S., Fengtai District
Telephone: 68384456, 68384457
Hours: 8:30-12:00, 13:30-17:00 (closed Saturdays & Sundays)
Admission: 30 Yuan; students, 15 Yuan
Public Transport: Take express public bus at Qianmen, get off at Liuyingmen station; or take bus No. 729

The China Space Museum has gathered all the major innovations in astronavigation, rockets, satellites, etc., in the realm of Chinese space flight. Covering a 5,000 sq. m area, the museum consists of the Introduction Hall, General Hall, Hi-tech Applications Hall, Specialized Division Hall.

The exterior of the China Space Museum

The museum presents the Long March series of carrier rockets and the DFH series of satellites, both representing landmarks in the development of China's space industry. It also displays various types of rocket engines and a large number of valuable photographs.

The re-entry cabin of the Shenzhou Spacecraft, exhibited in the center of the main exhibition hall

Rocket models developed through various periods of history

Dabaotai Western Han Dynasty Tomb Museum

Location: South of Guogong Village, Fengtai District
Telephone: 83613073
Admission: 20 Yuan; students, 10 Yuan
Hours: 9:00-16:00
Public Transport: Bus No. 744, 913, 944, 959

Covering an area of about 18,000 sq. m, the Dabaotai Western Han Dynasty Tomb Museum was built in the excavated underground palace of Liu Jian (73-45 BC), a prince of Guanyanqing in the Western Han Dynasty (206 BC-AD 25). The ancient tomb was built at the peak of the funeral rituals set up for Han emperors. Among the exhibits of the museum, the three carriages with red- spotted-wheels and black hoods and eleven horses are all real period objects, found buried in the tomb channel. The more than 1,000 relics unearthed include bronze ware, ironware, jade, agate, lacquer work, gold foil, pottery, and silk fabric. It is considered invaluable to the nation as the sole large-scale Han-dynasty tomb preserved completely at its original site, with the underground palace and the buried carriages and horses being of great value for the study of Han culture and the history of Beijing. There are also special programs uniquely designed to encourage the participation of visitors. For example, there are archeological research simulations and recreational activities about Han-dynasty culture.

Pottery figurines

The tomb built in the Western Han Dynasty

Wu Yunduo Memorial Hall

Location: East corner of Nanxiaojie intersection, Donggaodi, Fengtai District
Telephone: 67987065
Admission: 2 Yuan; students, 1.5 Yuan
Hours: 8:00-16:00 (closed Saturdays & Sundays)
Public Transport: Bus No. 341, 729, 742, 926

Wu Yunduo (1917-90), an expert on ordnance, was engaged in the study of artillery technology. During the War of Resistance against Japanese Aggression, under extremely difficult conditions he developed the manufacture of

Some items used by Wu Yunduo displayed in the main exhibition hall

powerful rifle grenades with launchers, as well as various types of mines and hand grenades. After New China was founded, he directed multiple projects including the study of recoilless artillery, anti-aircraft artillery and trench mortars. He also trained ordnance specialists, and made a great contribution to the modernization of China's national defense and improvement of equipment for the People's Liberation Aarmy.

The exterior of the Memorial Hall

With over 300 articles and photographs, the Memorial Hall displays the great contribution made by Wu Yunduo who, hailed as the "Pavel Korchagin of China," pioneered the cause of ordnance for the New China.

Lei Feng Memorial Hall

Location: East corner of Nanxiaojie intersection, Donggaodi, Fengtai District
Telephone: 67987065
Hours: 8:00-17:00 (closed Saturdays & Sundays)
Admission: Free
Public Transport: Bus No. 341, 729, 742, 926

An exhibition hall

A bust of Lei Feng

Since its foundation on August 1, 1977, and its opening to the public in March 1982, the Lei Feng Memorial Hall has continued to offer a free exhibition plus a mobile display to several Beijing districts and counties. Its regular exhibition has sections on "Lei Feng – Hero of Humanity," "Selected Lei Feng Speeches and Poems," "The Formation of the Lei Feng Spirit," "Content of the Lei Feng Spirit," "The Development of the Lei Feng Spirit," "Successors to the Lei Feng Spirit," "What Has Happened to the Lei Feng Spirit?" "The Study of the Lei Feng Spirit," "The Call of the Lei Feng Spirit," and "The Revitalization of the Lei Feng Spirit." The more than 1,000 items exhibited in these sections remind the public of the short but glorious life of Lei Feng, who grew from an ordinary soldier to a famed Communist warrior.

Memorial Hall for the February 7th Strike in Changxindian

Location: A15 Huayuan Nanli, west of Changxindian Railway Station, Fengtai District
Telephone: 83305948
Hours: 8:00-11:00, 13:30-17:30 (closed Sundays & Mondays)
Admission: Free
Public Transport: Bus No. 339, 917, 964

The Memorial Hall for the February 7th Strike in Changxindian was set up to commemorate an earth-shaking strike by workers at the Beijing-Hankou Railway Bureau from February 4 to 7, 1923. Formally opened to the public in 1987, this commemorative museum centers around an important event in China's revolutionary history. Its main exhibits include the iron monument cast for

The signal clock used by the strikers

the completion of the iron bridge across the Yellow River in the 31st year of the Guangxu reign of the Qing Dynasty (1905); the big clock that once hung in Changxindian Railway Station after the Beijing-Hankou Railroad was opened; the small cloth bag used to collect union membership dues in 1921; the badges of the Workers' Club in 1922; the siren used in the "August Strike"; the badges of the Beijing-Hankou Railroad Workers Union in

A mural in the Memorial Hall portraying railroad workers battling military policemen on February 7, 1923

1923; the ax and hammer handle used by members of the Workers Monitoring Team during the February 7th Strike; the handcuffs and fetters used on the arrested workers in Baoding Prison; and the timepiece and clock repair tools used by Shi Wenbin, a deputy head of the Preparatory Committee of the Beijing-Hankou Railroad Workers Union in 1923.

Beijing Liao and Jin City Wall Museum

Location: A40 Yulin Lane, Youanmenwai Avenue, Fengtai District
Telephone: 63054992
Hours: 9:00-16:00 (closed Mondays)
Admission: 10 Yuan; students, 5 Yuan
Public Transport: Bus No. 19, 49, 59, 122, 351, 716, 717, 744
Special bus route 3

Cizhou kiln jars dated from the Liao Dynasty

A section of the exhibition hall

The Beijing Liao (907-1125) and Jin (1115-1234) city wall was discovered and excavated in 1990, which was then turned into a museum and opened to the public in April 1995. A museum specializing in archeological studies, it consists of an underground section and a display. Visitors learn about the history of the city of Beijing from the Zhongdu period of the Jin Dynasty. The museum has preserved a water gate from the Yuan Dynasty – the largest of its kind among all the ancient city wall water-passes ever found in China. There are also many cultural relics dated from the Liao and Jin dynasties in the museum.

The ruins of the water gate at Zhongdu from the Jin Dynasty

Mentougou Museum

Location: 8 Mentougou Road, Mentougou District
Telephone: 69852446
Hours: 9:00-16:00 (closed Mondays)
Admission: 5 Yuan; students, 3 Yuan
Public Transport: Bus No. 101, 336, 370, 921, 931, 959

Founded in 1984, the Mentougou Museum was the first district-level museum built in the Beijing area. Mentougou was inhabited by humans as far back as the Neolithic Age. The museum displays the history, the revolutionary activities and the folk customs of the Mentougou District. The large number of articles and photographs exhibited in the museum reflect the evolution of the Mentougou region from ancient times.

The exterior of the Mentougou Museum

A tricolor Bodhisattva statue made in the Jiuquan Wu Kiln

Inside the exhibition hall

Museum of Peking Man Site at Zhoukoudian

> **Location:** Dragon Bone Mountain, Zhoukoudian, Fangshan District
> **Telephone:** 69301278
> **Hours:** 8:30-17:00
> **Admission:** 30 Yuan; students, 15 Yuan
> **Public Transport:** Bus No. 917, from Fangshan, change to loop bus route 2

Replica of the head of Peking Man

Contrasting skulls of a present-day ape, Peking Man and a modern human

The Museum of Peking Man Site at Zhoukoudian in Beijing founded in 1953 holds the world's richest collection of erect human fossils, fire use remains and cultural antiques of prehistoric civilization ever discovered. The exhibits systematically introduce the life and the living environment of "Peking Man," dated to

A reconstructed scene of Peking Men making a living

around 600,000 years ago, the New Cave Man of around 100,000 years ago, and the Upper Cave Man of around 18,000 years ago. The Peking Man Site at Zhoukoudian was listed under Cultural Relics Protection by the State Council of China in 1961, and registered in the List of World Cultural Heritage Sites by UNESCO in 1987.

The ruins of Peking Man in Zhoukoudian

The cave of Peking Man

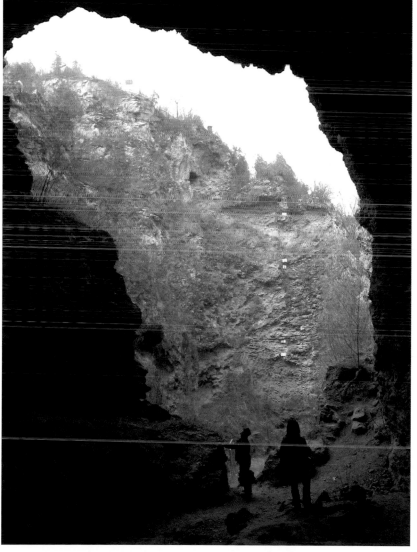

Museum of the Yan Capital Site of the Western Zhou Dynasty

Location: Dongjialin Village, Liulihe, Fangshan District
Telephone: 61393049
Hours: 8:30-16:30
Admission: 20 Yuan; students, 10 Yuan
Public Transport: Bus 917 (sub-route)

A cauldron

The Museum of the Yan Capital Site Museum of the Western Zhou Dynasty is located amidst ancient ruins from the Shang (1600-1046 BC) and Zhou (1046-256 BC) dynasties, whose relics are under national protection. Originally the ancient capital of the State of Yan, an important neighboring kingdom to the north of the Western Zhou Empire, the site bears the earliest testimony to the existence of the city of

The exterior of the museum

A container

Beijing more than 3,000 years ago. With a display of unearthed cultural relics on the original site of the ruins, the muscum focuses on archeological research. Its basic exhibition is entitled, "The Glorious Ancient Yan Capital Culture," illustrating the cultural panorama of the ancient Yan capital through a great number of historical relics from the Yan Kingdom of the Western Zhou period.

A square cauldron

Main exhibition hall

China Printing Museum

Location: 25 Xinghua Road N., Huangcun, Daxing District
Telephone: 60261237, 60261238
Hours: 8:30-16:30
Admission: 20 Yuan; students, 10 Yuan
Public Transport: Bus No. 410, 901, 937, 962, 968

The exterior of the China Printing Museum

A section of the exhibition hall

As the largest museum specializing in China's printing technology, the museum is located in the Beijing Printing Institute. Printing technology is one of the four great inventions of ancient China, and its development and dissemination has had a profound influence on human civilization and social progress in the world. The museum houses three specialized exhibition areas: "Ancient Printing," "Modern Printing," and "New Technology and Equipment." All together, they illustrate the Chinese history of printing, through the displays of all types of articles, pictures, texts and models.

A replica of woodblock and movable-type printing in the Qing Dynasty

Display of printing equipment used in old days

China Watermelon Museum

Location: Panggezhuang, Daxing District
Telephone: 89281181
Hours: 8:30-17:30
Admission: 20 Yuan; students, 10 Yuan
Public Transport: Bus No. 937

Located in Panggezhuang in Daxing District, an area famous for its watermelons, the China Melon Museum is the first specialized museum to focus on China's ancient melon culture. As Panggezhuang is situated on a fluvial plain of

China Watermelon Museum

the Yongding River, the area enjoys porous soil and obvious changes in diurnal temperature alongside ample sunshine. With these fine natural conditions, the area has become the largest producer of watermelons in the Beijing area. Shaped like a huge watermelon set off by two large green leaves, the museum's architecture is uniquely eye-catching. Named "a flying

Main exhibition hall

watermelon," its design motif symbolizes the soaring production of watermelon in Daxing. Inside the museum building is a vivid display of the history of watermelon cultivation, varieties of watermelon, and watermelon culture. The outdoor exhibition area of the museum has several dozen valuable watermelon varieties growing there. Visiting the museum in the summer,

A huge watermelon weighing 32.85 kg, grown by "Watermelon King" Song Baosen

visitors not only are able to learn more about watermelon cultivation, but also to taste various types of watermelon from around the world.

Beijing Nanhaizi Elk Park Museum

Location: Elk Park, Nanhaizi, Daxing District
Telephone: 87962105
Hours 8:00-18:00
Admission: Free
Public Transport: Bus No. 352, 377, 729, 750, from the Jiugong stop, take bus No. 736

Inscribed Reminders of Extinct Animals around the World

Occupying an area of nearly 66.6 ha, the Elk Park Museum is a conservation center dedicated to the protection of elk and other species of animals. It is also a base for popular science education for young people about animals and the environment. The sections of its exhibition include "The Life and Development of Elks," "Inscribed Reminders of Extinct Animals around the World," "Murals on Animal Protection in the East" and the "Hall of Deers of the World." Emphasizing humane considerations and participation by visitors, the museum is a valuable open classroom for learning open-field ecology.

Introduction to deers in an exhibition hall

Nanhaizi Elk Park

Dingling Tomb Museum

Location: The Ming Tombs, Changping District
Telephone: 60761424
Hours: 8:00-17:30
Admission: 60 Yuan; students, 30 Yuan
Public Transport: Tour bus routes 1, 2, 3, 4, 5, 9
Bus No. 345 to Changping, and transfer to bus No. 314

The Dingling Tomb Museum sits at the foot of Dayushan Mountain, 40 km north of Beijing. The tomb was constructed between the 12th and 18th years of the Wanli reign of the Ming Dynasty (1584-90). Occupying 180,000 sq. m, the tomb holds the remains of the Ming Emperor Wanli and his two empresses – Xiaoduan and Xiaojing. More than 3,000 rare treasures were excavated from the tomb. The most notable exhibits in the museum are the gold crown for the emperor, and the gold phoonix crown

The rear hall of the underground palace of the Dingling Tomb

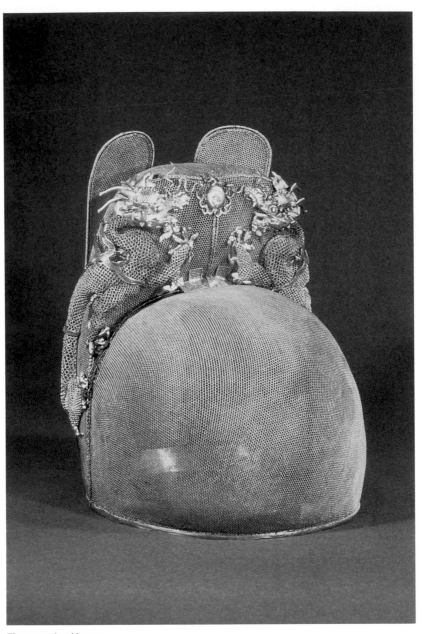

The emperor's gold crown

for the empress. The crowns were completely woven with thin gold wire and not even one connecting tie can be seen. A vivid design of two dragons playing with a big pearl is woven into the emperor's gold crown. As the only crown of this standard ever found in the country, it is a most precious cultural relic of China. The Dingling Tomb Museum

The empress' phoenix crown

houses two exhibition halls. One mainly holds visual and textual introductions to the original state of Dingling, and the process of the Dingling excavation. A large number of unearthed articles and relics, including portraits of the emperor and his empresses, the phoenix crowns, costumes and ribbons, are also on display. The other exhibition hall mainly holds funereal articles excavated from the underground palace.

The Dingling Tomb veiled in rain

China Aviation Museum

Location: West of Xiaotangshan Town, Changping District
Telephone: 61784882, 61784883
Hours: 8:00-17:30
Admission: 40 Yuan; students & seniors, 20 Yuan
Public Transport: Bus No. 912

An EWR aircraft converted from a TU-4 plane

An Il-18 plane once taken by Chairman Mao

Located in a large hangar dug into a mountain, the China Aviation Museum has collected over 200 aircraft models of various types. Many of these planes are valuable cultural artifacts in both national and international fields of aviation. The museum has also preserved more than 700 various models of anti-aircraft weapons and devices. It also shows films on air warfare and aviation knowledge. The China Aviation Museum is a top-level specialized museum on Chinese aviation.

China Aviation Museum

China Tank Museum

Location: West side of the highway to the north of Yangfang Town, Changping District
Telephone: 69767910, 66759901
Hours: 8:30-16:00
Admission: 18 Yuan; students, 5 Yuan
Public Transport: Bus No. 914, 330, get off at West Xiaoying stop, then take bus No. 911

The China Tank Museum was opened to the public on August 1, 1998. The 11 exhibition halls in the museum are grouped into 4 sections: "The History of Armored Corps," "Armored Tanks," "Simulated Tank Training Models," and "Simulated Weapon Samples." They illustrate how the Chinese army grew to strength from its first tank battalion founded in 1945 under the leadership of the CPC. The museum also exhibits a large number of tanks and armored vehicles, and often organizes rehearsals of tank obstacle races and tactical exercises.

Light tanks made in the USA

Exhibition hall

The China Tank Museum and a 96-MBT in front of the museum gate

Changping Museum

Location: East of Kangshan Square, Fuxue Road, Changping District
Telephone: 69741095
Hours: 8:30-16:30 (closed Mondays)
Admission: Free
Public Transport: Bus No. 345 (sub-route)

Funereal articles from the Liao Dynasty

A section of the exhibition hall

A bronze mirror engraved with a double-fish design, collected from the local people

The Changping Museum was established in 1988. Its main display, "Cultural Relics Unearthed in the Changping Region," offers a detailed introduction to valuable relics, dating to various Chinese dynasties, discovered in the Changping region in recent years.

Ancient pottery ware unearthed from Changping District

Shangzhai Cultural Exhibition Hall

Location: Jinhai Lake Tourist Area, Ping'gu District
Telephone: 69991268
Hours: 8:00-16:30
Admission: 5 Yuan; students, 3 Yuan
Public Transport: Bus No. 918 (sub-route)

Located in Shangzhai Village in Hanzhuang Township, Ping'gu District, the Shangzhai Cultural Exhibition Hall is a specialized museum built on the site of ruins. The natural and simple design of its exhibition hall merges well with its surrounding environment, giving visitors the feeling they have arrived at an ancient camp inhabited by a primitive tribe. The architectural structure of the main exhibition hall is patterned on a Guanchi cave-style saddle of the Neolithic Age. The two-storey museum occupies 1,284

The pottery bird-head pillar used in sacrificial ceremonies

The exterior of the Shangzhai Cultural Exhibition Hall

Decorative pottery item carved in a pig shape

sq. m. Its first floor displays "Shangzhai Culture" and its environment, as well as the archeological discoveries made in the region, illustrating the unique character of this culture, and gives a fairly comprehensive portrayal of the natural environment and the tribe's productive and social life through such unearthed items as axes, millstones, deep jars, bowls and cups. The second floor contains a general exhibition hall that mainly displays more than 200 cultural artifacts unearthed or collected in Ping'gu District over the past ten years, reflecting the life and production of the Ping'gu locals from ancient Shang and Zhou times until the Ming and Qing dynasties.

Inside the exhibition hall

Jiaozhuanghu Memorial Hall of a Tunnel Warfare Site

Location: Jiaozhuanghu Village, Longwantun Town, Shunyi District
Telephone: 60461906
Hours: 8:30-16:30
Admission: 30 Yuan; students, 15 Yuan
Public Transport: Take the express bus to Jiaozhuanghu at Dongzhimen

The new building of the Jiaozhuanghu Memorial Hall of a Tunnel Warfare Site was opened to the public on the eve of the 60th anniversary of the Chinese people's victory of the War of Resistance against Japanese Aggression. It occupies an area of 7,000 sq.m; and the floor space of the new museum building covers 2,000 sq.m. Originally founded in 1964, the Memorial Hall was built on the original site where Jiaozhuanghu villagers had dug tunnels in their fight against the Japanese invaders. A more than 600m-long tunnel is still extant today.

A former member of the Children's Brigade showing visitors the war loot they had captured from Japanese soldiers

The weapons used by militias of the time

A preserved underground bunker

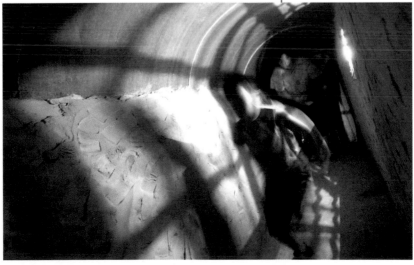

Museum of Chinese Militia Weaponry

Location: Jiaowangzhuang, Tongzhou District
Telephone: 89590788
Hours: 8:00-11:30, 14:30-16:00 (closed Mondays)
Admission: 30 Yuan; students, 15 Yuan
Public Transport: Bus No. 728, 846, 848

An iron cannon cast in the 20th year of the Daoguang reign in the Qing Dynasty

Various types of cannons once used by Chinese militiamen

Occupying a space of 8,600 sq. m, the exhibition area of the museum consists of the "Hall of Introduction," "Hall of the History of Chinese People's Militia," "Hall of Light Arms," "Hall of Artillery," among others. On display are all types of weapons and over 3,000 actual artifacts. The Hall of Light Arms exhibits over 1,200 pistols, rifles, submachine guns and other types of weapons made in over 20 countries. The Hall of Artillery has a 300mm gun-howitzer abandoned in northeastern China by the fleeing Japanese army.

The exterior of the museum

Tongzhou Museum

Location: 9 Western Avenue, Tongzhou District
Telephone: 69546442
Hours: 8:30-11:00, 14:00-17:00 (closed Mondays)
Admission: 1 Yuan
Public Transport: Bus No. 322, 342, 728, 848, get off at Xinhua Avenue

Completed and opened to the public in 1992, the Tongzhou Museum is located in a typical and well-preserved Beijing-style *siheyuan* with two sections built in the Qing Dynasty. Its basic exhibition is entitled "Ancient Tongzhou," and displays 164 valuable antiques unearthed from the Tongzhou region, illustrating its history over the past 2,200 years, after Tongzhou County was set up in the Western Han Dynasty, and portrays the enlightened and hardworking spirit of the local people.

Ancient iron anchors

Exhibition hall of the museum

Tongzhou Museum

Miyun Museum

Location: Inside Baihe Suburbs Park, Miyun District
Telephone: 69043124
Hours: 9:00-17:00 (closed Saturdays & Sundays)
Admission: 5 Yuan
Public Transport: Special bus from Dongzhimen to Miyun District

Exhibition Hall of Miyun History and Culture

A celadon vase

Located inside the scenic Baihe Suburbs Park in Mingyun, the museum specializes in the all-inclusive study of the social sciences and local topography. The former site of the museum was a princess' palace in the Qing Dynasty, sitting on the west side of the back street of the National Art Museum of China in the Dongcheng District. It moved to Miyun in 1985, and became the county museum of Miyun. Keeping its overall palatial structure, the museum has preserved the magnificent facade of a large grouping of ancient architecture. The permanent exhibitions in the museum include "Historical Antiques of Miyun" and "The Great Wall at Miyun."

The exterior of the Miyun Museum

The Great Wall Museum of China

Location: At the Badaling scenic site, Yanqing County
Telephone: 69121990, 69121830
Hours: 8:45-17:00
Admission: Covered by the full ticket to ascend the Great Wall
Public Transport: Bus No. 919

The Great Wall Museum of China was built at the foot of Badaling Mountain in Yanqing County, through where the Great Wall passes. Specializing in the past and present of the Great Wall, the museum has a display area of more than 3,000 sq. m. Its nine exhibition halls display: "The Great Wall Built through Various Dynasties," "The Great Wall in the Ming Dynasty," "Construction of Military Defenses," "Campaigns Conducted at the Great Wall,"

Eaves tile engraved with "Marriage between a Han princess and a king of the Xiongnu," from the Han Dynasty

The exterior of the Great Wall Museum of China

Reconstruction of an actual combat scene at the Great Wall, found in the main exhibition hall

Dragon-design bricks on the Great Wall built in the Ming Dynasty

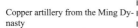

Copper artillery from the Ming Dynasty

"Economic and Cultural Exchanges," "A Treasure House of National Art," "Love China and Repair Our Great Wall," "The Champion of Scenic Sites," and "Rainbow of Friendship."

The exhibits in the museum include the "Certificate of World Cultural Inheritance," issued by the UNESCO, and photographs of over 200 state leaders from 120 countries who have climbed the Great Wall at Badaling.

A section of the exhibition hall

The Exhibition Hall of Shanrong Culture

Location: East of Yuhuangmiao Village, Zhangshanying Town, Yanqing County
Telephone: 69199534
Hours: 8:00-17:00
Admission: 5 Yuan
Public Transport: Bus No. 919, get off at Yanqing and take the local bus to the Shanrong Exhibition Hall

The Exhibition Hall of Shanrong Culture is the first exhibition hall named after an ancient ethnic minority in China. Its rich collection from archeological excavation displays the ancient cultural heritage of Shanrong – a powerful tribe active in the Yanshan Mountain region during the Spring and Autumn as well as the Warring States periods. There is a protective hall of about 400 sq. m built over an ancient graveyard scene in the museum. The 10 ancient graves in the protective hall include those of two tribal chiefs, five affluent tribal members and three commoners. Visitors learn of the funeral rites observed by the small Shanrong tribe in northern China during the mid and late Spring and Autumn Period. In combination with the replicas on display inside, there are outdoor grave pits to enable visitors to experience an archeological excavation. Replicas of human skeletons and funereal items, placed in the cleared Shanrong grave pits, give visitors the chance to enjoy the feel of an "archeological dig."

The exterior of the Exhibition Hall of Shanrong Culture

The numerous ancient tomb pits in the Exhibition Hall

The earliest and best-preserved bronze "hot pot" ever excavated in northern China

An unearthed gold-horse ornament

图书在版编目（CIP）数据

京城博物馆／兰佩瑾编；高明义等摄.
－北京：外文出版社，2006
（漫游北京）

ISBN 978-7-119-04387-6

Ⅰ．京… Ⅱ．①兰… ②高… Ⅲ．博物馆－简介－北京市－ 英文
Ⅳ．G269.271

中国版本图书馆 CIP 数据核字(2006)第 017582 号

编　　　辑：兰佩瑾
撰　　　文：子　慧
摄　　　影：王建华　高明义　乔建华　祝自祥　杨　茜　吴　江
　　　　　　张东伟　郭　群　唐　亮　朱　力　兰佩瑾　张肇基
　　　　　　CFP 图片库　观复古典艺术博物馆
翻　　　译：纪　华　高文星
英 文 定 稿：Kris Sri Bhaggiyadatta, May Yee, 王明杰
封 面 设 计：吴　涛
版 式 设 计：元　青等
印 刷 监 制：张国祥
责 任 编 辑：兰佩瑾

京城博物馆

© 外文出版社
外文出版社出版
（中国北京百万庄大街 24 号）
邮政编码：100037
外文出版社网页：http://www.flp.com.cn
北京外文印刷厂印刷
中国国际图书贸易总公司发行
（中国北京车公庄西路 35 号）
北京邮政信箱第 399 号 邮政编码 100044
2008 年(长 24 开)第 1 版
2008 年第 1 版第 1 次印刷
（英文）
ISBN 978-7-119-04387-6
13600 （平）
85-E-627P